The Epic History of Macaroni and Cheese

From Ancient Rome to Modern America

KARIMA MOYER-NOCCHI

Foreword by Paula J. Johnson

DIGGING INTO THE SURPRISING HISTORY OF AN EVER-POPULAR DISH

Today, macaroni and cheese is the ultimate comfort food, a staple of weeknight dinners, family gatherings, and Soul Food restaurants. Yet its history is filled with surprising twists and turns. Renaissance cardinals and popes dined on elaborate pasta-and-cheese concoctions laced with costly spices. In the eighteenth century, wealthy young Englishmen made macaroni a symbol of continental sophistication. Black women, whose contribution has long been overshadowed, played a crucial role in establishing the dish as an American tradition.

This book is a delectable history of macaroni and cheese, tracing an extraordinary journey of cultural exchange and social change. Karima Moyer-Nocchi reveals the religious, political, and industrial forces that shaped its evolution alongside stories of the unsung figures who crafted the dish as we know it today: enslaved cooks who preserved and adapted traditions, immigrant chefs who introduced new variations, and practical homemakers looking to nourish their families with an affordable meal. Deeply researched and rich with enticing details, this book uncovers the creativity and resilience that brought a beloved food to our tables. It also shares centuries of recipes—from ancient Roman authors to celebrity chefs—that provide a hands-on way to experience the evolution of this iconic dish.

KARIMA MOYER-NOCCHI is a culinary historian specializing in Italian food who teaches at the University of Siena. She is the author of *Chewing the Fat: An Oral History of Italian Foodways from Fascism to Dolce Vita* (2015) and *The Eternal Table: A Cultural History of Food in Rome* (2019).

PAULA J. JOHNSON is curator of food history at the Smithsonian National Museum of American History.

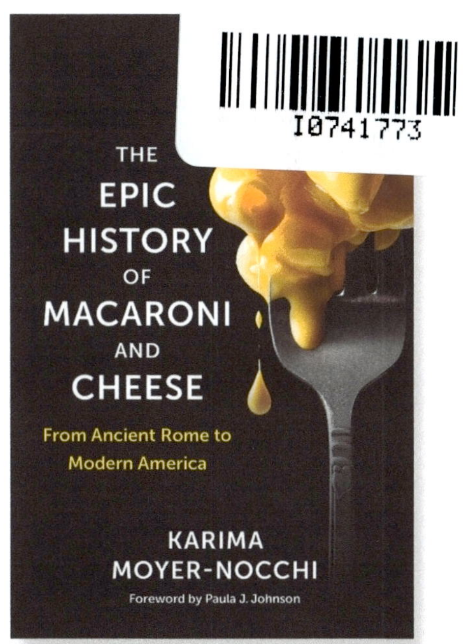

"Brilliant, indulgent, and impeccably researched. Moyer-Nocchi has crafted the definitive cultural biography of macaroni and cheese, tracing its journey across continents and through centuries with the precision of a historian and the warmth of a devoted cook. As a food scientist who's never outgrown my love for this dish, I savored every insight into how something so simple became so culturally profound. Whether your interest is scholarly or purely gastronomic, every page in this book immensely satisfies."

—Kantha Shelke, author of *Pasta and Noodles: A Global History*

$28.95t / £25.00 cloth 978-0-231-21531-2

FEBRUARY 368 pages / 6" x 9" / 34 b&w images; 8-page color insert

FOOD / HISTORY

ARTS AND TRADITIONS OF THE TABLE: PERSPECTIVES ON CULINARY HISTORY

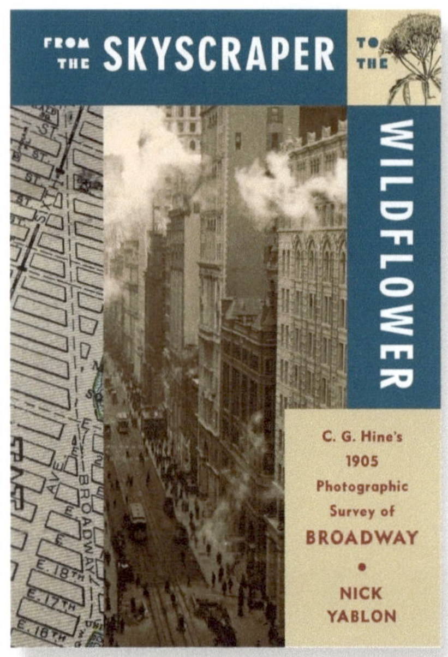

From the Skyscraper to the Wildflower

C. G. Hine's 1905 Photographic Survey of Broadway

NICK YABLON

TURN-OF-THE-CENTURY PHOTOGRAPHS OF BROADWAY THAT REVEAL A CHANGING CITY

Throughout 1905, an amateur photographer dedicated himself to capturing Broadway, from the bottom of Manhattan to the top. In sun, rain, and snow, at dawn and late at night, C. G. Hine depicted buildings that were threatened by rapid development: outmoded stores, hotels, and theaters, as well as workshops and shanties. His survey also foregrounded the street's other holdouts against change, such as sex workers, pushcart vendors, horses, and the trees and wildflowers of upper Manhattan. Hine ultimately assembled more than three hundred photographs, along with numerous newspaper clippings and a typed essay, into a three-volume album, titled "From the Sky Scraper to the Wild Flower."

Presenting striking images from Hine's album, this book offers a rare glimpse into the transformation of New York's built environment at the turn of the twentieth century. Nick Yablon explores Hine's connections to—and divergences from—movements and trends of the time, such as historic preservation, Pictorialist photography, botany, and bicycling. He curates a selection of Hine's photographs and investigates how they reveal deeper conflicts and tensions about urban development. *From the Skyscraper to the Wildflower* guides readers up Broadway block by block, casting light on New York's changing landscape, where signs of the modern clashed with vestiges of earlier eras.

"Deeply scholarly but highly readable, *From the Skyscraper to the Wildflower* is an in-depth exploration of a unique and personal historical artifact, offering new insights into the urban history of New York City."

—Joanna Merwood-Salisbury, author of *Barbarian Architecture: Thorstein Veblen's Chicago*

NICK YABLON is professor of history and American studies at the University of Iowa. He is the author of *Untimely Ruins: An Archaeology of American Urban Modernity, 1819–1919* (2009) and *Remembrance of Things Present: The Invention of the Time Capsule* (2019).

$50.00* / £42.00 paper 978-0-231-20353-1
$200.00 / £167.00 cloth 978-0-231-20352-4

APRIL 320 pages / 7" x 10" / 150 color photographs, 6 color maps

HISTORY / NEW YORK

Ignorance

What We Do Not Know, Cannot Know, Must Not Know, and Refuse to Know

GEORGE G. SZPIRO

WHAT WE CAN LEARN FROM LACK OF KNOWLEDGE

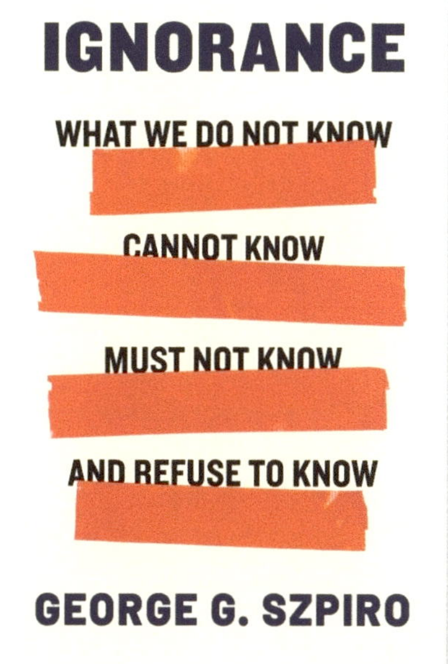

Does the lack of evidence mean that aliens don't exist? Why does an unproven mathematical hypothesis have profound consequences? Are humans capable of grasping the nature of divinity? Is it ethical to give a patient a placebo? Why do people persist in demonstrably false beliefs like flat earth theory? Should someone want to know when they will die?

George G. Szpiro examines these questions and many others, offering an engaging and witty tour of what we can learn from ignorance. In a series of fast-paced chapters, he unravels problems ranging across science, mathematics, law, economics, politics, religion, psychology, and philosophy—some esoteric, others drawn from everyday life. Ignorance comes in many forms, Szpiro shows. Some questions are only temporarily unsolved; others are inherently unanswerable. Sometimes authorities keep answers from us, for good or ill. Often our assumptions and biases keep us from overcoming our ignorance, and occasionally we choose to remain ignorant—for surprisingly rational reasons.

Ultimately, Szpiro argues, ignorance is not purely negative. It can motivate the pursuit of learning and wisdom—as long as we acknowledge it. Presenting sophisticated topics in an accessible way, this book shows how ignorance sheds light on the nature of knowledge.

"Szpiro returns with a witty, thought-provoking exploration of life, history, and the meaning of our existence. Fun to read yet deeply educational, this lively journey through ideas reminds us why books still matter."

—William Eimicke, Columbia University School of International and Public Affairs

GEORGE G. SZPIRO is an author and journalist who was a longtime correspondent for the Swiss daily *Neue Zürcher Zeitung*. His previous Columbia University Press books are *Risk, Choice, and Uncertainty: Three Centuries of Economic Decision-Making* (2020) and *Perplexing Paradoxes: Unraveling Enigmas in the World Around Us* (2024). Szpiro was on the faculty at the Wharton School, University of Pennsylvania, and the Hebrew University in Jerusalem.

$28.00* / £22.00 cloth 978-0-231-22165-8

MARCH 344 pages / 5.5" x 8.5" / 56 b&w figures

SCIENCE / PHILOSOPHY

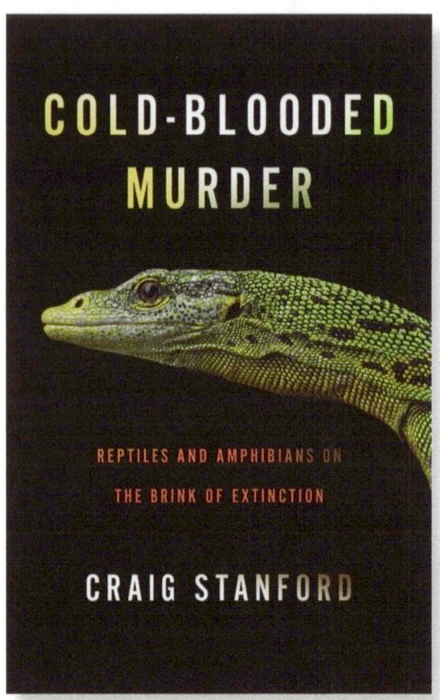

Cold-Blooded Murder

Reptiles and Amphibians on the Brink of Extinction

CRAIG STANFORD

THE STORIES OF SOME OF THE WORLD'S MOST THREATENED REPTILES AND AMPHIBIANS

Around the world, many reptile and amphibian species—from the iconic Komodo dragon to the unglamorous Telfair's skink—are facing grave threats. For many, like the Belalanda chameleon of Madagascar and Mexico's beloved axolotls, habitat destruction due to logging, agriculture, and development poses the greatest peril. Some, such as Galápagos giant tortoises, have been slaughtered wholesale by humans. Others, like Caribbean rock iguanas, have been driven to the brink of extinction by the introduction of new species to their island homes. Commercial exploitation is another risk to animals like the ploughshare tortoise, in high demand in the global black market pet trade. Still more, like Yosemite toads, face new threats as climate change accelerates.

Craig Stanford tells the captivating stories of dozens of endangered reptiles and amphibians, depicting the ecological roles and unique characteristics of each species. He takes readers on a globe-spanning journey, revealing the diversity and beauty of the creatures with whom we share our world. Stanford also highlights conservation projects that are protecting critically endangered animals, sharing inspiring success stories while acknowledging the difficulty of saving species. This gripping and poignant book shows why we should be fascinated by reptiles and amphibians—and strive to prevent their extinction.

"*Cold-Blooded Murder* is a beautifully written series of accounts about the rarest and most fascinating reptiles and amphibians on the planet, written by a well-known authority on the world's turtles and tortoises. I highly recommend it as a great natural history read."

—Russell A. Mittermeier, chief conservation officer, Re:wild

© ANDREA CURRYLOW

CRAIG STANFORD is professor of biological sciences at the University of Southern California. He is chair of the International Union for Conservation of Nature Tortoise and Freshwater Turtle Specialist Group and has conducted field studies of tortoises, turtles, and primates in South and Southeast Asia, East Africa, China, and Mexico. Stanford is the author of nineteen books, including *Planet Without Apes* (2014) and *The Last Tortoise: A Tale of Extinction in Our Lifetime* (2010).

$26.00* / £22.00 paper 978-0-231-22312-6
$110.00 / £92.00 cloth 978-0-231-22311-9
APRIL 208 pages / 5.5" x 8.5" / 9 b&w figures
SCIENCE

INTRODUCING THE WHAT SCIENCE SAYS SERIES

What Science Says is a collection of short books about subjects that are rife with misinformation and apparent controversy in public discourse but have a clear scientific consensus. Written by recognized experts in each field, these works are aimed at interested general readers. The books reveal the cultural and historical context in which disputed claims emerged, how they were scientifically tested, and what the results were.

What Science Says About Astrology

CARLOS ORSI

UNDERSTANDING THE APPEAL OF THE WORLD'S OLDEST SUPERSTITION

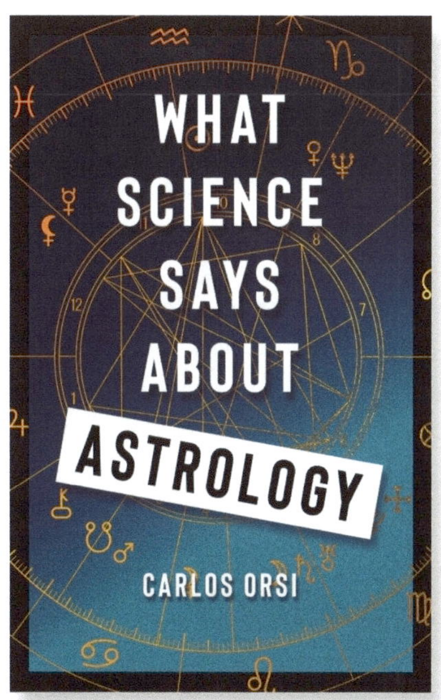

For thousands of years, people have believed that the configuration of stars and planets in the sky influences earthly events. Today, astrology is a lucrative global market, with newspaper columns, mobile apps, and professional counselors weighing in on everything from love life to health to the stock market. Yet scientific evidence shows indisputably that it is simply superstition. Why does astrology appeal to so many people? What makes its prognostications seem persuasive? Is there any harm to believing in astrology anyway?

This book aims a scientific lens at astrology, from its colorful history to experimental tests of its predictions through the social and psychological factors that explain its enduring popularity. Carlos Orsi explores the importance of astrology to the history of science and the reasons it has been categorized as a pseudoscience. He investigates its tenets, recounting how scientists debunked common claims. With both empathy and skepticism, Orsi illuminates the psychological, rhetorical, and emotional mechanisms that cause people to find astrological predictions convincing. He also addresses the dangers of irrational beliefs and the risks of applying astrology to serious decisions. Wide-ranging and entertaining, this book offers a critical look at the modern appeal of an ancient superstition.

"In this concise yet thoroughly authoritative volume, Carlos Orsi presents everything you need to know about the science of astrology. An entertaining and well-written account ranging from its ancient beginnings to its modern forms."

—Stuart Vyse, author of *Believing in Magic: The Psychology of Superstition*

© PAULO VITALE

CARLOS ORSI is an award-winning journalist with more than thirty years of experience in science writing.

$26.00* / £22.00 paper 978-0-231-22139-9
$110.00 / £92.00 cloth 978-0-231-22138-2

MAY 240 pages / 5.5" x 8.5"

SCIENCE

WHAT SCIENCE SAYS

How Film Became History

The Rise of the Archival Documentary in 1930s America

THOMAS DOHERTY

THE EARLY DOCUMENTARIES THAT RESHAPED OUR PERCEPTION OF WHAT FILM CAN DO

By the 1930s, filmmakers had access to a backlog of footage from around thirty years of motion pictures, allowing them to create a new kind of film stitched together from the raw material of older films. At the same time, the transition to synchronous sound added a transformative new element to the grammar of cinema: the voiceover narration. Together, the film inventory and offscreen commentary gave rise to the archival documentary, the motion picture genre that preserves and rewinds history.

Thomas Doherty tells the story of the archival documentary, spotlighting the first films that set out deliberately to preserve history on screen. He shows how newsreels and documentaries challenged the era's restrictive censorship and how film began to engage with the great political issues of the day. Doherty considers a range of films—some well-known, others obscure—including J. Stuart Blackton's *The Film Parade* (1933), Laurence Stallings and Truman Talley's *The First World War* (1934), Cornelius Vanderbilt Jr.'s *Hitler's Reign of Terror* (1934), Max Eastman and Herbert Axelbank's *Tsar to Lenin* (1937), and the *March of Time* screen magazine. Tracing the creation of the archival documentary, *How Film Became History* illuminates how motion pictures have come to shape our vision of the past.

"A richly detailed excavation of the forgotten documentaries of the 1930s—films that shaped culture, politics, and history in ways still felt today. Thomas Doherty once again proves himself a master historian of American cinema."

—Chris Yogerst, author, columnist, and media historian

THOMAS DOHERTY is professor of American studies at Brandeis University. His previous Columbia University Press books include *Hollywood and Hitler, 1933–1939* (2013); *Show Trial: Hollywood, HUAC, and the Birth of the Blacklist* (2018); and *Little Lindy Is Kidnapped: How the Media Covered the Crime of the Century* (2020).

$28.00* / £22.00 paper 978-0-231-22258-7
$110.00 / £92.00 cloth 978-0-231-22257-0

APRIL 264 pages / 6" x 9" / 33 b&w images

FILM AND MEDIA STUDIES

FILM AND CULTURE SERIES

I Hear Freedom

The Great Migration, Free Jazz, and Black Power

CISCO BRADLEY

Foreword by Gabriel Jermaine Vanlandingham-Dunn

AN ORAL HISTORY OF THE ROOTS OF FREE JAZZ

Around the 1960s, a musical revolution took place in the industrial landscapes of Cleveland and Detroit. Disenchanted with the strictures of bebop, musicians forged a new style—free jazz—that took inspiration from a vast range of sources, including figures such as Ornette Coleman, Cecil Taylor, and John Coltrane; African and Middle Eastern music; avant-garde modernism; and the politics and aesthetics of Black Power. How did this radical movement come about, and what explains its creativity and vitality?

Based on interviews with dozens of musicians, *I Hear Freedom* tells the story of free jazz and its connection to the broader Black experience. Cisco Bradley demonstrates that free jazz is deeply rooted in the musical traditions and aesthetics that the Great Migration brought from the South. As postwar urban renewal projects fractured Black communities, musicians drew on this heritage to create new forms of expression. Figures such as Albert Ayler, Donald Ayler, Charles Tyler, Frank Wright, Bobby Few, Charles Moore, and Faruq Z. Bey developed distinct artistic visions, often influenced by their involvement in Black liberation movements. *I Hear Freedom* chronicles the Cleveland and Detroit free jazz scenes, and it follows musicians to New York, Los Angeles, Paris, and beyond. A revelatory oral history, this book shows that free jazz is a uniquely Black style shaped by mobility, community, and the struggle for freedom.

CISCO BRADLEY is professor of history at the Pratt Institute. His books include *The Williamsburg Avant-Garde: Experimental Music and Sound on the Brooklyn Waterfront* (2023) and *Universal Tonality: The Life and Music of William Parker* (2021). He is also the director of the documentary *Take Me to Fendika* (2024).

GABRIEL JERMAINE VANLANDINGHAM-DUNN is a music historian, writer, researcher, and DJ who heads cow: Music and is the creative consultant at Astral Spirits Records.

"Cisco Bradley guides readers through an alternative, ethnographic model of jazz—and thus American music—history. Other jazz scholars posit linear genealogies, with musicians/composers evolving out of past styles and artists; Bradley instead situates Black improvising musicians/composers within their familial, community, and professional networks. With extensive and unprecedented archival research, Bradley reveals how migratory movement drove free jazz's experimentalist praxis and how encounters made along the journey culminated in art."

—Kwami Coleman, author of *Change: The New Thing and Modern Jazz*

$32.00* / £28.00 paper 978-0-231-22157-3
$140.00 / £117.00 cloth 978-0-231-22156-6

MARCH 480 pages / 6.125" x 9.25" / 30 b&w illustrations

MUSIC / BLACK STUDIES

BLACK LIVES IN THE DIASPORA: PAST / PRESENT / FUTURE

Recipes for the Melting Pot

The Lives of The Settlement Cook Book

NORA L. RUBEL

AMERICAN JEWISH WOMEN'S LIVES AS REFLECTED THROUGH A PERENNIALLY POPULAR COOKBOOK

In 1901, Lizzie Black Kander put together a cookbook based on the classes she taught at the Milwaukee Jewish Mission. "I was trying to teach a group of young foreign girls in a crowded neighborhood how to cook simple and nutritious food, yet have it attractive and inexpensive as we prepare it in America," she recalled. *The Settlement Cook Book* would go on to be the most successful charitable cookbook in American history, remaining a best-seller into the 1970s. Despite including nonkosher recipes, it became a mainstay in Jewish kitchens and an enduring touchstone of Jewish American culture.

Recipes for the Melting Pot tells the remarkable story of *The Settlement Cook Book*, demonstrating how it shaped Jewish American identity—and was in turn shaped by generations of Jewish women. Nora L. Rubel traces the cookbook's evolution across forty editions over several decades, through waves of immigration, shifting gender roles, upward mobility, suburbanization, and rapid changes in Jewish life. She argues that the book celebrates pluralism, allowing it to serve at once as a tool for Americanization, a repository of tradition, and a platform for culinary innovation. Ultimately, *The Settlement Cook Book* is a record of American Jewish women's history, told through the food they made and the lives they led. A cultural biography of an iconic cookbook, this lively and inviting book shares an inclusive vision of American cuisine.

"For someone obsessed with 'The Settlement' since childhood, Rubel's book is a dream come true, answering my every question about the life of Lizzie Black Kander, the juxtaposition of kosher and treyf, the provenance of the recipes, and the community and society in which the book came forth and flourished."

—Bonnie Slotnick, owner of Bonnie Slotnick Cookbooks

"In this well-written and thoroughly researched book, Rubel provides a new perspective on American Jewish life through the lens of a widely used yet rarely studied volume: *The Settlement Cook Book*."

—Rebecca Alpert, professor of religion emerita, Temple University

NORA L. RUBEL is the Elizabeth Denio Professor in Jewish Studies at the University of Rochester. She is the author of *Doubting the Devout: The Ultra-Orthodox in the Jewish American Imagination* (Columbia, 2009), as well as coeditor of *Religion, Food, and Eating in North America* (Columbia, 2014) and *Blessings Beyond the Binary:* Transparent *and the Queer Jewish Family* (2024).

$28.00* / £22.00 paper 978-0-231-22434-5
$110.00 / £85.00 cloth 978-0-231-16394-1
JUNE 240 pages / 6" x 9" / 11 b&w illustrations
FOOD HISTORY / JEWISH STUDIES

On Taste

In Humans and Other Animals

DAVIDE RISSO AND GABRIELLA MORINI

Translated by Elettra Pauletto

AN ENGAGING EXAMINATION OF TASTE AND FLAVOR BY TWO EXPERT SCIENTISTS

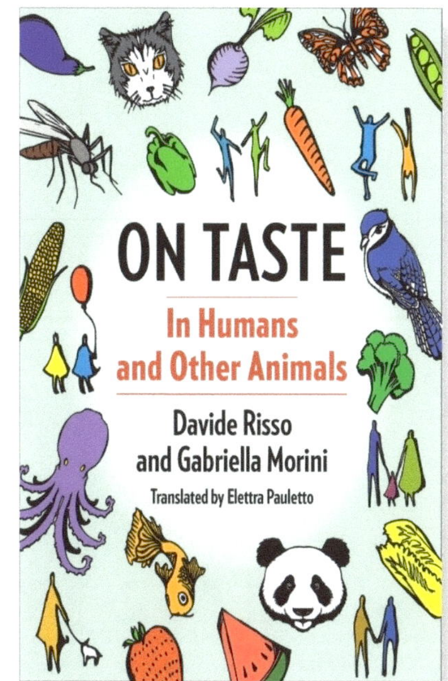

Are there only five tastes, sweet, salty, sour, bitter, and umami? Why are some so appealing while others are what we call acquired tastes? Do other animals perceive tastes in the same way humans do? How did the sense of taste evolve? Should the hotness of chili peppers, the coolness of mint, and the pungency of garlic be considered tastes? What can taste teach us about our health and our environment?

In this book, two leading researchers take readers on a lively journey through the science of taste. Davide Risso and Gabriella Morini trace its evolution across millions of years, ranging from microbes to octopuses through birds and finally humans. They explain how taste receptors allow us to decode the chemical composition of food and distinguish between edible and toxic items. Evolution has given varied species different capabilities, so pandas lack the ability to taste umami and cats do not perceive sweetness. *On Taste* also reveals how mosquitoes choose their prey—and why they like some people more than others. Rigorous and accessible, this book shows how taste unlocks the connections between science and culture, letting us understand our foods and our world more richly.

DAVIDE RISSO is a molecular biologist who specializes in taste and nutrition science. He received a PhD from the University of Bologna, and he has held research roles for major international food companies.

GABRIELLA MORINI is assistant professor of taste and food sciences at the University of Gastronomic Sciences of Pollenzo, Italy, and scientific director of the Pollenzo Food Lab. She is also a visiting scientist in the Department of Food Science at the University of Copenhagen.

"A fascinating and beautifully detailed study, *On Taste* combines scientific rigor with genuine curiosity. Risso and Morini reveal the intricate ways our senses connect us to the world, offering insights that will intrigue food lovers and science enthusiasts alike."

—Demet Güzey, author of *Mustard: A Global History*

$22.00* / £17.99 cloth 978-0-231-22129-0

APRIL 112 pages / 5.5" x 8.5"

FOOD SCIENCE

ARTS AND TRADITIONS OF THE TABLE: PERSPECTIVES ON CULINARY HISTORY

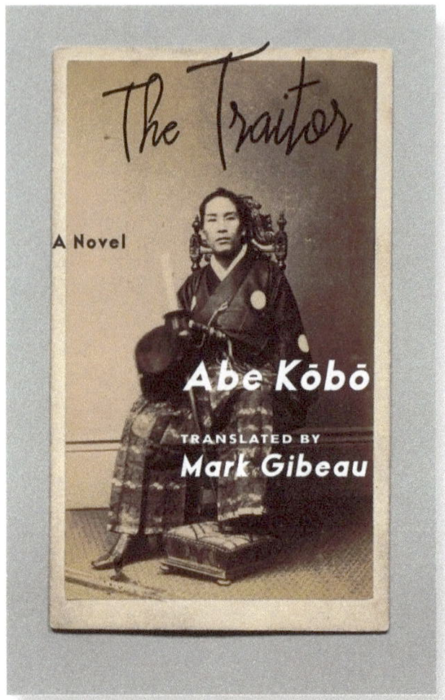

The Traitor

A Novel

ABE KŌBŌ

Translated by Mark Gibeau

A NOVEL ABOUT THE PITFALLS OF LOYALTY BY AN ICONIC JAPANESE WRITER

In postwar Japan, a writer meets a small-town innkeeper who is obsessed with a tale from the nineteenth century. He relates the saga of Enomoto Takeaki, an admiral in the final years of the Tokugawa shogunate who regained authority under the Meiji government. A former member of imperial Japan's military police, the innkeeper dwells on the question of loyalty even as he struggles with his responsibility for the arrest and murder of his brother-in-law during the war. Later, he sends the writer a mysterious manuscript purporting to be the account of a peddler turned samurai whom Enomoto betrayed.

Part historical fiction, part detective story, *The Traitor* is a remarkable novel about navigating changing political landscapes by one of the most significant modern Japanese writers. In his only historical novel, Abe Kōbō turns to a pivotal moment in Japan's past to explore profound questions about the nature of loyalty and the choices that people must make when they encounter forces beyond their control or understanding. Published in 1964, when a new generation had begun asking their parents about the war, Abe's tale of betrayal sparked controversy across the political spectrum. The great writer's most important previously untranslated novel, *The Traitor* displays Abe's literary mastery from a new angle.

ABE KŌBŌ (1924–1993) was one of Japan's greatest postwar writers, acclaimed for his imaginative fiction and plays of the absurd. Among his best-known novels are *The Woman in the Dunes*, *The Face of Another*, and *The Box Man*.

MARK GIBEAU has translated the novel *A Shameful Life* by Dazai Osamu (2018), as well as works by Kawabata Yasunari, Tanizaki Jun'ichirō, and Miyamoto Yuriko, among others.

"Abe Kōbō's novels were prescient . . . and they still are. What could be more timely for us than this prescient historical novel in a masterful translation!"

—Roger Pulvers, author of *My Japan: A Cultural Memoir*

$26.00* / £20.00 paper 978-0-231-21295-3
$105.00 / £81.00 cloth 978-0-231-21294-6

MARCH 384 pages / 5.5" x 8.5" / 4 b&w illustrations

FICTION IN TRANSLATION

Eyes of the Sky

SYAMAN RAPONGAN

Translated by Kyle Shernuk

A VIVIDLY WRITTEN MULTIGENERATIONAL ECOLOGICAL INDIGENOUS NOVEL

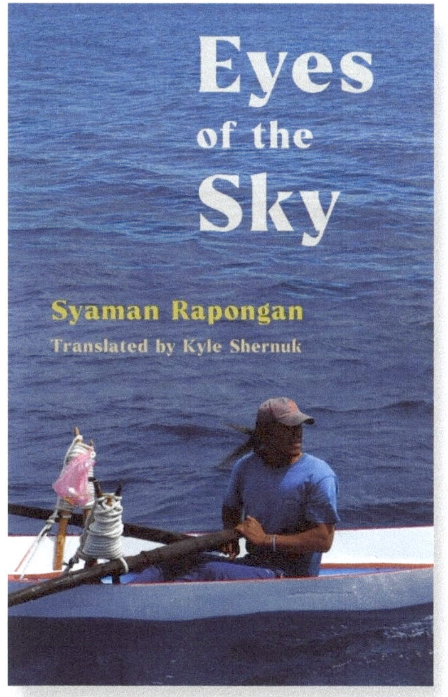

Syaman Rapongan is a chronicler of his people, the Tao, an Indigenous community who live on Orchid Island near the island of Taiwan. In *Eyes of the Sky*, he invites readers to learn the ways of this oceanic world—and to learn to see their own worlds anew through a Tao lens.

Employing oral storytelling conventions, *Eyes of the Sky* opens by recounting the history of the Tao, from their mythic origins to the present day. Its first chapter is narrated by a giant trevally, a fish common to the waters around Orchid Island. It then tells the stories of three generations of a single family—father, son, and grandson—exploring the transformation of Tao society through their encounters with Han-Taiwanese modernity.

Syaman Rapongan paints a vivid picture of his homeland—its mountains and seas, flora and fauna, climate and ecology—as well as local culture and customs. In describing fishing practices, canoe building, and conversations with friends from his village, he illustrates the Tao's ecological worldview, lived experience, and struggle to preserve their culture. Written in conversational prose with evocative detail, this book is a powerful testament to how Indigenous people and stories persevere.

SYAMAN RAPONGAN is an acclaimed Tao writer who lives on Pongso no Tao or Orchid Island. He is the author of many books, including *Eyes of the Ocean*, published in English translation by Columbia University Press. Syaman Rapongan is a tireless advocate for Tao culture, an expert diver, and a master canoe carver.

KYLE SHERNUK is assistant professor of modern Chinese literature and culture at Georgetown University.

"The translation of Syaman Rapongan's *Eyes of the Sky* at last allows Anglophone readers to see one of the most important Indigenous works of literature from the western Pacific. This is a universal tale of devotions and regrets, songs and stories, about multispecies interdependence, generational continuities, Indigenous-settler relations, and the wondrous moments where flying fish scales shimmer like stars that are the eyes of the sky."

—Shu-mei Shih, coeditor of *Indigenous Knowledge in Taiwan and Beyond*

$25.00* / £22.00 paper 978-0-231-21171-0
$100.00 / £82.00 cloth 978-0-231-21170-3

MARCH 224 pages / 5.5" x 8.5" / 8 b&w figures

LITERATURE IN TRANSLATION

MODERN CHINESE LITERATURE FROM TAIWAN

World English-language Rights: Columbia University Press; All Other Rights: National Museum of Taiwan Literature

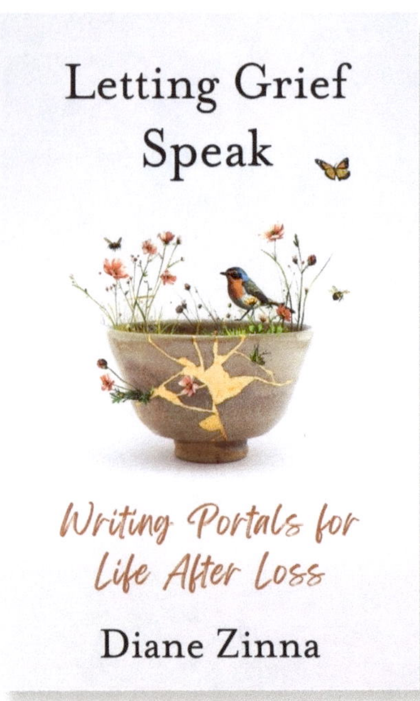

Letting Grief Speak

Writing Portals for Life After Loss

DIANE ZINNA

A PROMPT-BASED GUIDE TO WRITING ABOUT LOSS

Society doesn't always make it easy to tell stories about loss. Grief can make us feel that we have crossed over to another side, where people can't reach us and we can't reach others. We're encouraged to move quickly through the often-misunderstood "stages of grief"; we fear that we are burdening others with our pain. But pain can feel more manageable when we find ways to describe it—and writing about grief can help us connect with others who have felt pain of their own.

Letting Grief Speak is a creative writing craft book on the art of telling our hardest stories. Based on a class called Grief Writing Sundays that Diane Zinna has led for several years, it provides ninety writing prompts with accompanying craft techniques to help people find language for their grief. By turns gentle, unexpected, rebellious, and wonderfully strange, these prompts open portals: entryways into spaces where difficult emotions can become meaningful narratives. Warm, sensitive, and honest, *Letting Grief Speak* is a memoir of the craft, interwoven with stories from the author's own life. It also includes pieces from acclaimed writers and more than forty of her Grief Writing students, inviting readers to find their own ways to tell vulnerable stories. A tool for writers and a companion for grievers, this book meets writers of all levels where they are, no matter what kind of grief they hold.

"*Letting Grief Speak* is a gentle, careful, solid guide for anyone approaching the work of writing loss. Zinna collects stories, her own and others, and provides writing portals to help people communicate their grief. She pushes back against the idea that we are isolated in our sorrow, teaching us how to make our stories both personal and universal."

—Eiren Caffall, author of *The Mourner's Bestiary*

© JOSEFIN WALDEN

DIANE ZINNA is the author of *The All-Night Sun* (2020), which was longlisted for the Center for Fiction's First Novel Prize. Her work has appeared in *Brevity*, the *Bellevue Literary Review*, and *CutBank*. A Pushcart Prize nominee, she has taught creative writing for more than twenty years.

$28.00* / £22.00 paper 978-0-231-21269-4
$110.00 / £85.00 cloth 978-0-231-21268-7

JUNE 408 pages/5.5"x8.5"

CREATIVE WRITING

Interracial Marriage

How Diverse Couples Navigate Relationships in a Divided Time

GEOFFREY L. GREIF, VICTORIA D. STUBBS, AND MICHAEL E. WOOLLEY

A LARGE-SCALE STUDY OF CONTEMPORARY INTERRACIAL RELATIONSHIPS

The rate of interracial marriage in the United States has steadily increased: One in six new marriages now crosses racial or ethnic lines. Yet these partnerships are not always embraced or even accepted by families, friends, and society. Within families, issues ranging from food and holiday traditions to parenting approaches and beliefs about gender roles sometimes must be negotiated between cultures. In a time of national division, questions of race and identity have become deeply fraught.

This book—based on interviews with and surveys of hundreds of people and informed by the authors' many decades of experience as therapists and researchers—explores how intermarried couples build lives together. People of varied backgrounds describe how they navigate a world where others wonder about their relationship, question the parentage of their children, and treat them differently from their partner based on their appearance. They speak candidly about the joys and challenges of raising mixed-race children. Many of these couples have strengthened their relationships by learning to communicate across cultural barriers, and they share strategies for overcoming misunderstandings. At once large-scale and intimate, this book offers practical advice and timely insight into the triumphs and struggles of love across lines of difference.

GEOFFREY L. GREIF is Distinguished University Professor at the University of Maryland School of Social Work and a licensed clinical social worker.

VICTORIA D. STUBBS is the founder of Inner Truth Psychotherapy and Wellness and was previously a full-time clinical instructor at the University of Maryland School of Social Work.

MICHAEL E. WOOLLEY is a retired professor at the University of Maryland School of Social Work. He is coauthor, with Greif, of *Adult Sibling Relationships* (Columbia, 2016).

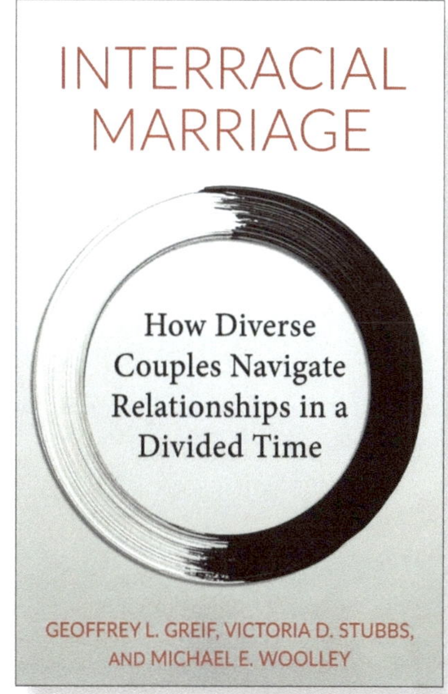

"This book's key strength is its big heart. *Interracial Marriage* is a compassionate exploration of a topic that many might wish to ignore or gloss over. Drawing on therapeutic expertise and lived experience, the authors offer strategies that will benefit readers dealing with differences in close relationships as well as readers interested in race and ethnic relationships in American society."

—Pam Sheff, Johns Hopkins University

$28.00* / £22.00 paper 978-0-231-21818-4
$110.00 / £92.00 cloth 978-0-231-21819-1

MAY 280 pages / 5.5" x 8.5"

SOCIAL WORK / PSYCHOLOGY

Socially Wired

How Culture Shapes Our Brains

MATTHEW W. SCHELKE

WHAT NEUROLOGY REVEALS ABOUT CULTURAL EXPERIENCE

From birth, our brains are shaped by other people—in our families, schools, workplaces, neighborhoods, countries, and cultures. These social worlds make us who we are, but how this process works remains mysterious on a neural level.

In *Socially Wired*, Matthew W. Schelke uses the stories of patients with neurological illness to show how social and cultural environments transform the brain. In the neurology clinic, the experiences of patients with the same illness can vary tremendously depending on their backgrounds, providing a window onto the complex interactions between brain and culture. Through cases ranging from an amateur chef who suddenly stopped cooking to an art lover who was removed from a gallery for touching the art, Schelke explores what neurological injury can reveal about social and cultural behavior. He demonstrates how specific practices—shared emotion, apprenticeship learning, imagination, language, art, and collective memory—shape neural networks, the experiences of patients, and ultimately our encultured minds.

Going beyond neuroscience, *Socially Wired* integrates insights from anthropology to philosophy to ecological psychology. Highlighting patient stories, this book illuminates how the brain wires us to participate in culture and how, in turn, culture rewires the brain.

"*Socially Wired* reimagines neurological processes as a deeply cultural experience, blending science and imagination to reveal how our understanding of the brain is shaped by the societies we live in—and how culture itself can transform the way we think about our minds."

—Daniel Yon, Birkbeck, University of London

MATTHEW W. SCHELKE is a general neurologist at Columbia University Irving Medical Center and the Neurological Institute of New York, where he sees patients with a wide range of neurological illnesses. He has published articles on the connections between neurology, neuroscience, and social and cultural life.

$28.00* / £22.00 paper 978-0-231-22227-3
$110.00 / £85.00 cloth 978-0-231-22226-6

JUNE 288 pages / 5.5" x 8.5" / 3 b&w figures

SCIENCE

The World Inside Your Head

How Perceptions Build Society

CHARLES MAURER AND DAPHNE MAURER

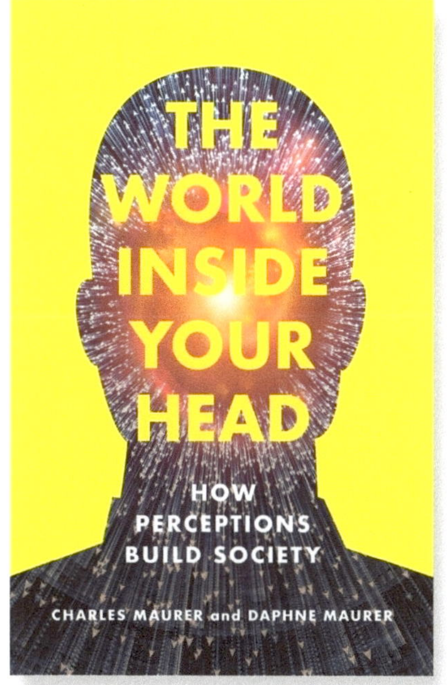

UNDERSTANDING THE NEURAL MECHANISMS THAT SHAPE PSYCHOLOGY AND SOCIETY

To socialize, your brain needs to see and hear other people, yet it is sealed inside a bony box: your skull. How does an internal mass of tissue comprehend the world outside? How does it form social relationships? This groundbreaking book answers those questions and reveals the perceptual underpinnings of society.

Charles and Daphne Maurer provide a clear explanation of how the brain interprets sensory inputs, showing how rudimentary sensations evolve into social interactions at every scale from nursery to nation. Their novel approach shows how sights, sounds, and smells build social and political worlds. They offer fresh insights into broad swaths of the social sciences.

The World Inside Your Head brings science to life, interweaving cutting-edge research with eye-opening examples across cultures and eras. Its style is lively and free of jargon, yet its argument is rigorous and scholarly. It is an accessible and iconoclastic rethinking of conventional psychology.

CHARLES MAURER is a science writer whose work includes two other groundbreaking books with Daphne Maurer about perception, *The World of the Newborn* (1988), which received the Book Award of the American Psychological Association, and *Pretty Ugly: Why We Like Some Songs, Faces, Foods, Plays, Pictures, Poems, Etc., and Dislike Others* (2019).

DAPHNE MAURER is a Distinguished University Professor at McMaster University in the Department of Psychology, Neuroscience, and Behaviour.

"This engaging and accessible book explores how complex human behaviors emerge from simple neural and social processes. Using neuroscience, psychology, and quantum theory, the authors reveal how perception, adaptation, and context shape learning, bias, and social norms to rethink the roots of individuality, conformity, and collective behavior."

—Emmanuel Pothos, City St. George's, University of London

$25.00* / £20.00 paper 978-0-231-22348-5
$100.00 / £84.00 cloth 978-0-231-22347-8

JUNE 200 pages / 5.5" x 8.5" / 8 b&w figures, 2 tables

SCIENCE

Connection

How Technology Can Make Us Better Humans

DAN TURELLO

"Thrilling and fun. From Aristotle and Dante to Bono and adrienne maree brown, Dan Turello takes us to a wonderland where technology meets ideas."

—Azar Nafisi, *New York Times* best-selling author of *Reading Lolita in Tehran: A Memoir in Books*

Dan Turello offers a philosophical and literary meditation on what technology is and can be, arguing that it provides surprising ways to strengthen and deepen what makes us human. Putting medieval Italian poets and Renaissance artists in conversation with contemporary philosophers and pop culture, this book traces the roots of our fascination with—and aversion to—technology. Turello shows how the moments that shaped Western views of technology offer perspective on our current predicaments.

DAN TURELLO is a writer, cultural historian, and photographer. His work has appeared in the *Washington Post*, *Psyche*, and the *Los Angeles Review of Books*, among others.

$25.00* / £20.00 paper 978-0-231-22016-3
$100.00 / £78.00 cloth 978-0-231-22015-6

MARCH 248 pages / 5.5" x 8.5" / 2 b&w photographs

PHILOSOPHY

NO LIMITS

Marginality

Solidarity and the Fight for Social Change

JIN Y. PARK

"A compassionately incisive meditation on the cries and creativity of the marginalized. As personal as it is philosophical, *Marginality* weaves real and fictional life stories and experiences into a compelling call to action."

—Peter D. Hershock, author of *Consciousness Mattering: A Buddhist Synthesis*

This groundbreaking book reimagines marginality as a transformative force, interweaving personal narratives with cultural, literary, and philosophical analysis to reveal how perspectives from the margins can catalyze social change. Drawing on her own experiences as an Asian American female philosopher specializing in non-Western thought, Jin Y. Park argues that personal stories are essential to philosophical inquiry.

JIN Y. PARK is William Fraser McDowell Chair Professor of Philosophy and Religion at American University. She has served as president of the American Academy of Religion, the North American Korean Philosophy Association, and the Society for Asian and Comparative Philosophy.

$22.00* / £17.99 paper 978-0-231-20937-3
$90.00 / £75.00 cloth 978-0-231-20936-6

AVAILABLE NOW 184 pages / 5.5" x 8.5"

PHILOSOPHY

NO LIMITS

Nietzsche

Anti-Philosophy 1

ALAIN BADIOU

Translated by Bruno Bosteels with Susan Spitzer

Introduction by Bruno Bosteels

ALAIN BADIOU'S HIGHLY ORIGINAL READING OF NIETZSCHE

For Alain Badiou, Friedrich Nietzsche is the "prince" of anti-philosophy. French leftist thinkers celebrated Nietzsche in the second half of the twentieth century, but when a backlash emerged in the 1990s, Badiou refused to join the attack. Instead, Badiou devoted his 1992–1993 seminar to an astonishingly original reading of Nietzsche—to whom he had previously shown indifference or scorn—in which he appears almost enamored with the author of *The Anti-Christ* and *Ecce Homo*.

This book presents Badiou's seminar on Nietzsche's late works, which for the first time addresses what would become one of his central concepts: anti-philosophy and its adversarial yet intimate relationship with philosophy. For Badiou, Nietzsche is the key modern anti-philosopher, his antagonist—and occasional ally—in the battle to redefine the work of philosophy. Badiou takes for granted Nietzsche's declaration that "God is dead," yet he rejects Nietzsche's assertion that philosophy too is past its expiration date. Badiou engages a century-long tradition of grappling with Nietzsche's paradoxes, considering thinkers such as Heidegger, Deleuze, and Derrida. Examining Nietzsche's impassioned writings on Wagner, he reflects on the nature of art and aesthetics. Provocative and profound, this seminar shows Badiou's ongoing project of reasserting the value of philosophy from a new angle.

"This book supplies a completely novel interpretation of the importance of Nietzsche's philosophy for the contemporary world. In Badiou's examination of his late writings, Nietzsche ceases to be just a worthy antagonist for Badiou's thought and becomes instead a valuable ally in his philosophical project. What emerges here is a breathtaking exploration of Nietzsche that departs from all the received wisdom."

—Todd McGowan, author of *Pure Excess: Capitalism and the Commodity*

ALAIN BADIOU is one of the most important philosophers of our time. He is emeritus professor of philosophy at the École normale supérieure in Paris. His seminars published by Columbia University Press include *Images of the Present Time* (2023) and *Parmenides* (2025).

BRUNO BOSTEELS is dean of humanities and Jesse and George Siegel Professor in the Humanities in the Department of Latin American and Iberian Cultures at Columbia University.

SUSAN SPITZER is a frequent translator of Badiou's works.

$35.00 / £30.00 cloth 978-0-231-18130-3

MAY 376 pages / 5.5" x 8.5"

PHILOSOPHY

THE SEMINARS OF ALAIN BADIOU

Gianni Vattimo

Philosopher, Communist, Catholic, Nihilist

THOMAS JARED FARMER

THE FIRST INTELLECTUAL BIOGRAPHY OF ITALIAN PHILOSOPHER OF RELIGION GIANNI VATTIMO

Gianni Vattimo (1936–2023) was among the most significant Italian philosophers of the last fifty years. A controversial figure both at home and abroad, he sometimes described himself paradoxically as a "nihilist" and as a "communist Catholic." Despite his provocations—and unusually for an academic philosopher—he served two terms in the European Parliament. For decades, Vattimo was at the forefront of developments in continental philosophy, spanning hermeneutics, postmodernity, and the "return to religion." Drawing on the work of figures such as Heidegger, Marx, Nietzsche, Gadamer, Rorty, and Kuhn, Vattimo constructed his signature concept of "weak thought," a way of approaching the persistent problems of ideology, violence, and social division after the so-called end of metaphysics.

In this book, Thomas Jared Farmer provides a groundbreaking examination of Vattimo's life and work. He considers the distinctive contributions that Vattimo made to postmodern thought as well as to recent debates in political philosophy and religion. This book provides an accessible introduction to Vattimo's overall philosophical project while also contextualizing it through discussions of important intellectual figures, key events in Italian history, and details about his personal trajectory. Authoritative and comprehensive, it is an indispensable companion to the works of one of the most original thinkers to emerge in the second half of the twentieth century.

"Gianni Vattimo's thought continues to inform some of the most important discussions of contemporary philosophy and religion. With this groundbreaking intellectual biography, Farmer provides not only a comprehensive overview of Vattimo's life and work but also an insightful interpretive analysis. You can't really know Vattimo unless you read it."

—Clayton Crockett, University of Central Arkansas and Global Centre for Advanced Studies

THOMAS JARED FARMER is the McDonald Scholar in Residence at the Center for the Study of Law and Religion at Emory University School of Law.

$30.00* / £25.00 paper 978-0-231-21892-4
$120.00 / £100.00 cloth 978-0-231-21891-7

AVAILABLE NOW 400 pages / 5.5" x 8.5"

PHILOSOPHY

Jürgen Habermas

Public Intellectual and Engaged Critical Theorist

PETER J. VEROVŠEK

UNDERSTANDING JÜRGEN HABERMAS THROUGH HIS WRITING FOR THE PUBLIC

Jürgen Habermas is Germany's most important postwar philosopher, the leading figure of the Frankfurt School in this period. He is best known for the concept of the public sphere, which forms the basis of his communicative understanding of democratic politics. Habermas has not only theorized the public sphere—he has also taken part in it through frequent commentary on current social, political, and cultural issues. Yet since Habermas's extensive public-facing writings have been overlooked, his philosophy has often been criticized as apolitical.

This book transforms our understanding of Habermas by focusing on his work as a public intellectual, showing how he has shaped debates far beyond the ivory tower. Peter J. Verovšek argues that while Habermas maintains a strict separation between his academic and his public-facing writings, these two aspects of his work are part of a consistent whole. The book highlights the development of Habermas's views over time and the changing nature of his interventions. Verovšek sheds light on the interrelationship between Habermas's participation in the public sphere and his theoretical work, demonstrating that his political engagement is crucial to understanding his philosophy. In a moment when public debate is under threat, this book offers timely new insight into Habermas's lifelong project of defending the public sphere—both in theory and in practice.

"This book is an extraordinary accomplishment, bringing together nearly seven decades of Habermas's journalistic writings with his theoretical work to cast new light on both. Drawing on Habermas's newly collected archives, Verovšek illuminates Habermas's unique understanding of the public intellectual as a democratic citizen who is at once an irritant to public discourse and a synthesizer of inchoate cultural and social trends."

—Seyla Benhabib, professor emerita, Yale University, and senior research scholar, Columbia Law School

PETER J. VEROVŠEK is senior assistant professor in history and theory of European integration at the University of Groningen. He is the author of *Memory and the Future of Europe: Rupture and Integration in the Wake of Total War* (2020).

$40.00* / £35.00 paper 978-0-231-21303-5
$160.00 / £134.00 cloth 978-0-231-21302-8

MARCH 448 pages / 6.125" x 9.25"

PHILOSOPHY

NEW DIRECTIONS IN CRITICAL THEORY

The Language of Terrorists

Distinguishing Trolls from Violent Extremists

JULIA EBNER

WHEN DOES ONLINE HATE SPEECH LEAD TO REAL-WORLD VIOLENCE?

If someone posts a death threat or a violent manifesto online, will they cross over from words to deeds? Explicit threats, intimidation campaigns, and incitements to violence are no rarity among white nationalists, incels, and other racist and misogynist extremists. Yet it is often difficult to determine whether they pose genuine risks, since the boundaries between trolling and true violent intent can be blurry. How can we tell the difference between online bluster and terrorist threats?

Julia Ebner—an internationally acclaimed expert on online radicalization—offers a fresh approach, showing how language patterns reveal the potential for political violence. She investigates the psychological underpinnings of texts by terrorists such as Anders Breivik, Dylann Roof, Elliot Rodger, and Brenton Tarrant, offering statistical and qualitative contrasts with nonviolent political writing. Ebner finds striking similarities among their manifestos, including the fusion of personal identity with the group, visceral othering of outgroups, narratives of existential conflict, and the glorification of violence. Following these trails, she demonstrates that perpetrators of extremist violence inadvertently give away their intentions in what they say. Featuring vivid writing and actionable conclusions, *The Language of Terrorists* presents a new model of violent threat detection that can address pressing challenges faced by the international security and intelligence communities.

JULIA EBNER is the leader of the Violent Extremism Lab at the University of Oxford's Centre for the Study of Social Cohesion and co-executive director at the Institute for Strategic Dialogue. She regularly advises governments, intelligence agencies, tech firms, and international organizations. Her books include *Going Dark: The Secret Social Lives of Extremists* (2019) and *Going Mainstream: How Extremists Are Taking Over* (2023).

"When is a joke just a joke, and when might it signal the next attack? Combining the rigors of anthropology and data analysis with a steely eye on multiple unfolding terrorist threats, Julia Ebner breaks new ground in separating the signal from the noise. Essential reading for threat analysts everywhere."

—John Horgan, author of *Terrorist Minds: The Psychology of Violent Extremism from Al-Qaeda to the Far Right*

"A must-read for anyone who wants to understand the roots of violent extremism."

—Harvey Whitehouse, author of *Inheritance: The Evolutionary Origins of the Modern World*

$28.00* / £22.00 paper 978-0-231-21441-4
$110.00 / £85.00 cloth 978-0-231-21440-7

JULY 304 pages / 6" x 9" / 6 b&w illustrations

SECURITY STUDIES

COLUMBIA STUDIES IN TERRORISM AND IRREGULAR WARFARE

China's Weaponization of Trade

Resistance Through Collective Resilience

VICTOR D. CHA, ELLEN KIM, AND ANDY LIM

HOW COUNTRIES CAN RESIST ECONOMIC COERCION

In recent years, China and the United States have each turned economic interdependence into an instrument of coercion, using their dominant positions in international trade to push states and firms to comply with their political goals. What is distinctive about this form of economic pressure, and how can other countries fight back?

This groundbreaking book explores the weaponization of economic interdependence and its implications for the international order through a wealth of new and original data on China's economic statecraft. Victor D. Cha, Ellen Kim, and Andy Lim examine how and in what ways the United States and China have deployed economic coercion, focusing on China's extensive use of this tactic over the past three decades. They analyze a vast data set that includes more than 600 cases of China's economic bullying of states, companies, and individuals in North America, Asia, and Europe. Cha, Kim, and Lim propose a multilateral strategy of "collective resilience" to counter intimidation, showing how targeted states can band together, leverage trading relationships, and threaten retaliation.

Synthesizing new insights from unique trade data with international security expertise, this timely book sheds new light on how China exercises economic power—and it provides a playbook to deter bullies and rebalance the global order.

VICTOR D. CHA is Distinguished University Professor and D. S. Song-KF Endowed Chair in Government and International Affairs at Georgetown University as well as president of the Geopolitics and Foreign Policy Department and Korea Chair at the Center for Strategic and International Studies. He is a former director for Asian affairs on the White House National Security Council.

ELLEN KIM is director of academic affairs at the Korea Economic Institute of America.

ANDY LIM is deputy director and fellow with the Korea Chair at the Center for Strategic and International Studies.

"Cha, Kim, and Lim have provided a fascinating account of how China has used its vast and intertwined trade networks to advance its own interests—and use these same commercial ties to undermine the industries and businesses of its global rivals. They also offer essential recommendations about how like-minded nations can band together to create collective resilience in the face of China's sustained challenge."

—Kurt M. Campbell, former US deputy secretary of state and Indo-Pacific coordinator at the National Security Council (2021–25)

$30.00* / £25.00 paper 978-0-231-22240-2
$120.00 / £100.00 cloth 978-0-231-22239-6

JANUARY 408 pages / 6.125" x 9.25" / 5 b&w illustrations

POLITICS

CONTEMPORARY ASIA IN THE WORLD

Song Jiaoren

A Republican Revolutionary and the Fate of Democracy in China

DON C. PRICE

THE LIFE, WORK, AND TRAGIC DEATH OF A LITTLE-KNOWN CHINESE LEADER

Song Jiaoren (1882–1913) was early-twentieth-century China's greatest champion of constitutional democracy. Fleeing the police after a failed plot in 1904, the young revolutionary found refuge in Japan, where his eyes were opened to new political possibilities. Along with Sun Yatsen, he was one of the founders of the Nationalist Party, turning an underground organization into a nationwide force. After the 1911 revolution, Song campaigned for a truly democratic constitution guaranteeing a representative government. Following parliamentary elections in 1913, on the verge of becoming prime minister, he was struck down by an assassin's bullet on a Shanghai railway platform, and China began its descent into chaos and authoritarianism.

Don C. Price provides the definitive biography of Song Jiaoren, recounting his remarkable career and illuminating a period of epochal change. Drawing on a wide variety of sources—especially his revealing diary—this book chronicles Song's life and times, interweaving his personal relationships with his revolutionary activities and intellectual development. From his early life in a rural interior province to his Japanese exile through his meteoric ascent and tragic death, it explores how Song became an unwavering advocate for democracy—and why antidemocratic forces sought to eliminate him. By detailing Song's legacy, this book sheds light on the roots of democratic aspirations in China and on the path not taken in the country's tumultuous history.

DON C. PRICE is professor emeritus of history at the University of California, Davis. He is the author of *Russia and the Roots of the Chinese Revolution, 1896–1911* (1974) and a coeditor of *Beyond the May Fourth Paradigm: In Search of Chinese Modernity* (2008), among other publications on Chinese history.

"This book is a testament to Price's encyclopedic knowledge of Song Jiaoren: the man, his family, and the intellectual and political milieux to which he belonged."

—Brian Tsui, author of *China's Conservative Revolution: The Quest for a New Order, 1927–1949*

$35.00* / £30.00 paper 978-0-231-22385-0
$140.00 / £117.00 cloth 978-0-231-22117-7

JUNE 512 pages / 6.125" x 9.25" / 24 b&w illustrations

HISTORY

Black Arts, Black Muslims

Islam in the Black Freedom Struggle

ELLEN McLARNEY

THE FOUNDATIONAL ROLE OF ISLAM IN THE BLACK ARTS MOVEMENT

In the late 1960s and early 1970s, prominent figures in the Black Arts Movement (BAM) converted to Islam and took new names. Poets such as Amiri Baraka, Sonia Sanchez, Askia Muhammad Touré, and Marvin X incorporated Islamic words and expressions, references to the Qur'an, and Arabic script, as well as symbols like the crescent star and depictions of Islamic architecture and clothing. They connected places like Harlem, Chicago, Newark, and Oakland to locales in the Muslim world such as Timbuktu, Songhai, and Mecca. These artists also played a pivotal role in developing Black studies and creating alternatives to the Eurocentrism of the American educational system.

Ellen McLarney explores how BAM writers identified with Islam as integral to the African American cultural, spiritual, and intellectual heritage. Examining poetry, visual art, music, drama, and mixed-media collaborations, she traces the emergence of a new kind of Islamic art rooted in the African American experience. Their works protested scientific racism, police brutality, colonial domination, and economic oppression while resurrecting a suppressed Islamic past and sharing spiritual visions of a new kind of future. Based on interviews, fieldwork, archival research, and close analysis of key works, this book reveals how BAM redefined Black art, Islamic poetics, and Black Muslim aesthetics in the struggle for racial justice.

ELLEN McLARNEY is associate professor of Middle East, Arabic, and African and African American studies at Duke University. She led a project on Muslim American poets and musicians of African descent with the Doris Duke Foundation for Islamic Art as well as an initiative on Islam and racial justice in the American South. She has also published in *Souls*, *The Black Scholar*, and *Black Perspectives*.

"McLarney uniquely and adeptly places multiple versions and interpretations of Islam, and self-identified Muslims, at the core of the Black Arts Movement and related movements. All future scholarship on not just the Black Arts Movement but also Black studies and Black Power will have to contend with *Black Arts, Black Muslims*."

—Michael O. West, coeditor of *From Toussaint to Tupac: The Black International Since the Age of Revolution*

$32.00* / £28.00 paper 978-0-231-21942-6
$130.00 / £109.00 cloth 978-0-231-21941-9

MARCH 384 pages / 6.125" x 9.25" / 13 illustrations

BLACK STUDIES

BLACK LIVES IN THE DIASPORA: PAST / PRESENT / FUTURE

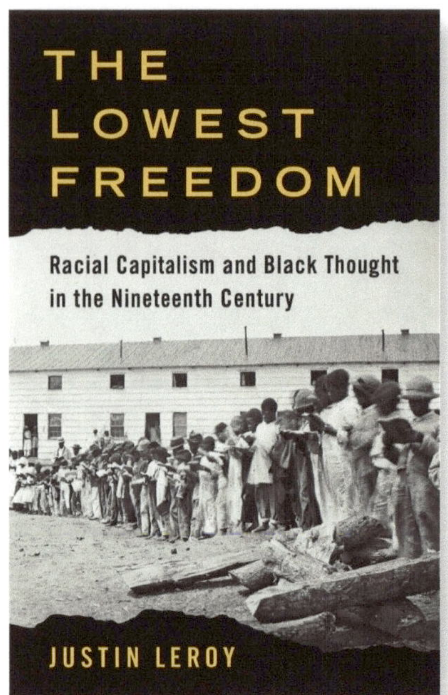

The Lowest Freedom

Racial Capitalism and Black Thought in the Nineteenth Century

JUSTIN LEROY

HOW THE BLACK RADICAL TRADITION EXPLORED THE LIMITS OF FREEDOM UNDER CAPITALISM

Throughout the nineteenth century, Black thinkers grappled with the material limits of freedom. They insisted that emancipation without economic self-determination would reproduce the inequalities of slavery, arguing that true freedom required not only civil rights and suffrage but also defending the rights of workers and curbing the power of capital. They concluded that free Black life could not flourish in conditions of labor exploitation and economic deprivation.

The Lowest Freedom is an intellectual history of how economic dispossession shaped the meaning of freedom in Black thought from antebellum abolitionism to the rise of Jim Crow. Justin Leroy argues that figures such as Frederick Douglass, T. Thomas Fortune, Maria Stewart, David Walker, and Ida B. Wells developed a critique of racial capitalism that remains underappreciated. Their theories spanned the eras of slavery and freedom, connecting the North and the South, by illuminating the political economy of racial domination and the interwoven relationship between race and capitalism. By situating their work within broader debates about land, labor, and capital, Leroy provides a new framework for understanding how freedom was theorized, contested, and ultimately constrained in the aftermath of slavery. Bridging Black studies, intellectual history, and the history of capitalism, *The Lowest Freedom* offers a reinterpretation of African American political thought that places the struggle for economic justice at its core.

JUSTIN LEROY is assistant professor of history at Duke University. He is coeditor of *Histories of Racial Capitalism* (Columbia, 2021).

"Through its unique excavations of the Black radical tradition's critiques of US freedom, *The Lowest Freedom* provides a radical rethinking of Black freedom and racial capitalism in the nineteenth-century United States."

—Zach Sell, author of *Trouble of the World: Slavery and Empire in the Age of Capital*

$27.00* / £22.00 paper 978-0-231-22356-0
$110.00 / £85.00 cloth 978-0-231-18198-3

APRIL 264 pages/5.5"x8.5"

HISTORY

COLUMBIA STUDIES IN THE HISTORY OF U.S. CAPITALISM

Coding Capitalism

Computers and the Remaking of the Postwar US Economy

DEVIN KENNEDY

THE COMPUTER'S ROLE IN US CAPITALISM

Long before Google, Amazon, or Microsoft, computer technology shaped how people worked, how markets operated, and how businesses became big. After World War II, military officials and their partners in industry looked to the newly invented electronic computer as they sought to cut costs, speed up labor, manage supply chains, and—they hoped—bring stability to the postwar economy. Their efforts would shape early computer science and the first applications of computer technology in manufacturing and business, with profound consequences for workers and managers alike. By the 1960s, practices originally developed to improve industrial efficiency were being used by Wall Street. Digital technology became central to finance, tying together far-flung trading floors and automating decision making—with alarming consequences, including the 1987 Black Monday crash.

Devin Kennedy offers a new history of the digital economy, showing how the computer emerged from—and transformed—capitalism in the United States. He traces how computer science and technology were made by industry, which molded computation to manage factories, financial markets, and entire firms. Drawing on the archives of businesses, computer researchers, regulators, and financial institutions, *Coding Capitalism* retells the story of the postwar economy and the computer, revealing how midcentury business laid the foundations of the digital world. Bridging business and economic history with the history of science and technology, this book uncovers the prehistory of big tech and demonstrates how capitalism has shaped computing since its invention.

DEVIN KENNEDY is assistant professor of history and the Evelyn and Herbert Howe Bascom Professor of Integrated Liberal Studies at the University of Wisconsin–Madison.

"*Coding Capitalism* is a remarkable achievement: an impressive, synthetic overview of forty years of computational practices in industry, management science, and finance. For historians of computing, business, and finance, this book will connect many dots."

—Paul N. Edwards, author of *A Vast Machine: Computer Models, Climate Data, and the Politics of Global Warming*

$30.00* / £25.00 paper 978-0-231-22403-1
$120.00 / £100.00 cloth 978-0-231-20114-8

JULY 320 pages / 6" x 9" / 12 b&w illustrations

HISTORY

COLUMBIA STUDIES IN THE HISTORY OF U.S. CAPITALISM

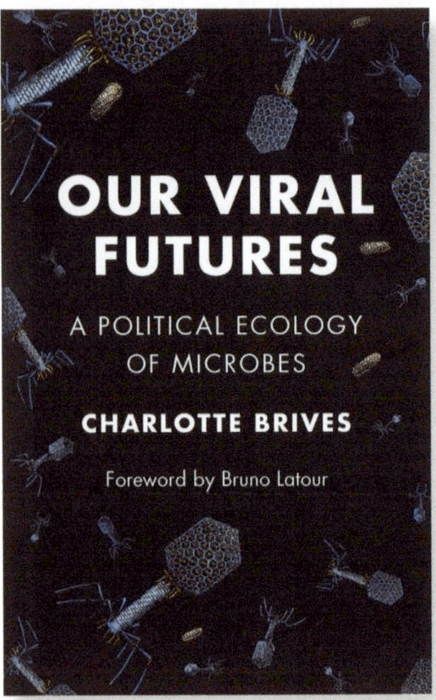

Our Viral Futures

A Political Ecology of Microbes

CHARLOTTE BRIVES

Foreword by Bruno Latour

A NEW COURSE FOR HUMAN RELATIONSHIPS WITH THE MICROBIOLOGICAL WORLD

Increasing bacterial resistance to antibiotics is one of today's greatest threats to public health. Yet a possible solution has emerged from a surprising source. Phage therapy deploys viruses called bacteriophages, "bacteria eaters," to treat infections. What concerns—both biological and social—arise from using viruses in this way? What does phage therapy reveal about the links between humans and microbes?

In *Our Viral Futures*, Charlotte Brives examines the development and implications of this therapy, providing new ways to understand our interconnections with the microbial world. Considering patients seeking treatment for chronic infections, the establishment of new regulatory frameworks, and the processes of laboratory research and clinical trials, she highlights the complexity and variety of the relationships among humans, phages, and bacteria. Brives places phage therapy in the context of the widespread use of antibiotics under industrial capitalism, which has enabled ecologically devastating forms of mass production and consumption. She argues that the connections between human societies and microbial communities defy the usual categories through which science and medicine understand the world, giving rise to new moral and political questions. Interdisciplinary and nuanced, *Our Viral Futures* poses a provocative challenge: Instead of continuing to assert that we can control and master microbes, we must learn to coexist with them.

"How shall we best live with viruses? This fascinating book tells the story of bacteriophages, therapeutically promising viruses that kill—or reenergize—bacteria. Emerging only in the relation, they challenge regulatory boards even as they open mysteries at the borders between life and nonlife. Brives draws us into both challenge and mystery."

—Anna Lowenhaupt Tsing, coauthor of *Field Guide to the Patchy Anthropocene: The New Nature*

CHARLOTTE BRIVES is an anthropologist of science and biomedicine. She is director of research at the Centre national de la recherche scientifique (CNRS).

BRUNO LATOUR (1947–2022) was among the most important figures in science and technology studies.

$35.00* / £30.00 paper 978-0-231-22198-6
$140.00 / £117.00 cloth 978-0-231-22197-9

FEBRUARY 280 pages / 5.5" x 8.5" / 17 b&w illustrations

SOCIOLOGY

SCIENCE NOW

Intertwined Creatures

The Embodied Cognitive Science of Self and Other

ANTHONY CHEMERO

WHY THE SELF IS FUNDAMENTALLY SOCIAL

In one common view, the mind is immaterial, internal, and invisible. From this perspective, the mind is inherently individual and isolated: It is unknowable from the outside, separated from the world and from other minds. Anthony Chemero—both a philosopher and a cognitive scientist—offers a powerful challenge to this theory of mind. Bringing together philosophical insight and empirical data, he develops a new understanding of the mind that centers embodiment and social interaction.

According to Chemero, the mind is intertwined with the world: It depends on the body, the surrounding environment, and the people with whom an individual interacts. He shows that cutting-edge research in cognitive science provides striking experimental evidence for this concept of the intertwined self. Chemero explores the philosophical, moral, and political implications of the claim that the self is necessarily interwoven with the world and with others, drawing connections to phenomenology, critical theory, and feminist political theory. Deeply interdisciplinary and engagingly written, *Intertwined Creatures* makes an urgent case for seeing the self as social—especially in the age of AI—with radical consequences for ethics and politics.

ANTHONY CHEMERO is University Distinguished Research Professor of Philosophy and Psychology at the University of Cincinnati. He is the author of *Radical Embodied Cognitive Science* (2009) and coauthor of *Phenomenology: An Introduction* (second edition, 2021).

"In an age where AI is the zeitgeist, the individual brain is a computer, and thinking is computation, Anthony Chemero provides a compelling rebuttal—backed by empirical research and dynamical systems modeling—that favors what he calls the intertwined self. Chemero leads an impressive group of philosophers and scientists who conceive of a mind centered on embodiment, environment, and other members of the human species. Those seeking an antidote to AI, or at least a complement of it, should take a dose of *Intertwined Creatures* as soon as possible. They won't regret it."

—Scott Kelso, author of *Dynamic Patterns: The Self-Organization of Brain and Behavior*

\$30.00* / £25.00 paper 978-0-231-22319-5
\$120.00 / £94.00 cloth 978-0-231-19538-6
MARCH 256 pages / 5.5" x 8.5" / 10 b&w illustrations
PHILOSOPHY

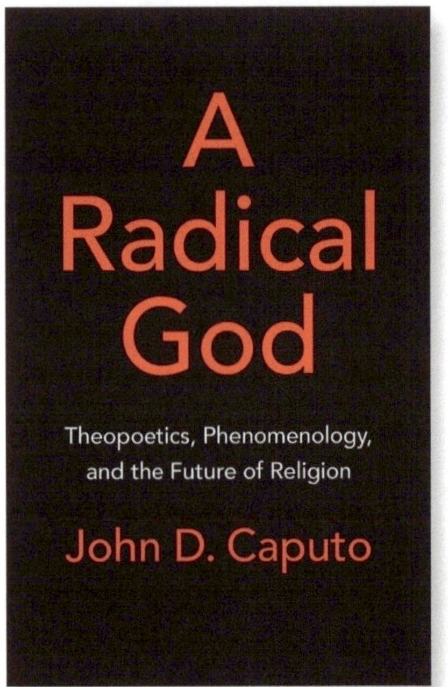

A Radical God

Theopoetics, Phenomenology, and the Future of Religion

JOHN D. CAPUTO

WHY GOD EMERGES FROM THE POETIC IMAGINATION

Religion is making itself unbelievable—scandal-ridden, antiscientific, authoritarian, and reactionary. Can religion be saved? Is it even worth trying to save religion, not just from its critics but from itself?

John D. Caputo proposes a radical alternative—what he calls "religion's last stand"—by turning to theopoetics. In the traditional account, theopoetics calls for approaching God poetically because God transcends human language. Caputo contests this view, arguing that in the radical account, God does not precede but is generated by the poetic imagination. Theopoetics is not adorning an already constituted God; it is constituting the very idea of God. A radical God, untethered from theological orthodoxy and confessional rivalries, is neither a real being nor an unreal illusion, neither the object of supernatural belief nor the reject of skeptical disbelief. By adopting a phenomenological suspension of both belief and disbelief, both theism and atheism, both the religious and the secular, Caputo demystifies the distinction between the natural and the supernatural and replaces it with the distinction between the prosaic and the poetic. A daring undertaking in radical theology, this lively and provocative book proposes a startlingly different future for religion.

"Caputo has produced something truly novel in the modern history of philosophy and religious studies, demonstrating that attention to the method of phenomenology leads not merely to more philosophy or theology but to a theopoetics, and thus to the possibilities of a God beyond God. *A Radical God* rewards readers willing to stay with Caputo's invitation to join him in an intellectual and philosophical exploration."

—Scott Holland, Bethany Theological Seminary

© KATHRYN ROBERTS

JOHN D. CAPUTO is the Thomas J. Watson Professor Emeritus of Religion and Humanities at Syracuse University and the David R. Cook Professor Emeritus of Philosophy at Villanova University. His most recent books are *What to Believe? Twelve Brief Lessons in Radical Theology* (Columbia, 2023) and *Specters of God: An Anatomy of the Apophatic Imagination* (2022).

\$35.00* / £30.00 paper 978-0-231-22364-5
\$140.00 / £117.00 cloth 978-0-231-22363-8

JUNE 488 pages / 5.5" x 8.5"

RELIGION

Kaleidoscope

Pluralism, White Supremacy, and American Religious History

CATHERINE L. ALBANESE

THE CLASH OF WHITE SUPREMACY AND RELIGIOUS MULTICULTURALISM ACROSS AMERICAN HISTORY

There is an abiding tension in American religious history—and in how that history is told—between the pervasive ideology of white supremacy and the reality of a multicultural, multireligious North American landscape. Visiting this tension from the colonial era to the present, Catherine L. Albanese explores collisions between a white Protestant majority and the diversity of faiths flourishing beside it, offering timely insights into transformations in American religion.

Beginning with how Indigenous peoples felt the heavy hand of settler violence, *Kaleidoscope* examines coexistence and conflict across American history in a series of essays. Albanese considers a number of moments and movements in Anglo-American Protestant religiosity even as she looks to Native, Black, and Latinx spiritual traditions. She highlights the uncertain status of Catholics and Jews, following their quest for whiteness and acceptance, and shows how Mormons too asserted their place within the United States by extolling their whiteness.

Filled with rich detail and a varied cast of characters, *Kaleidoscope* offers a new lens on diversity within American religious history. Elegantly written and powerfully argued, this book calls for overturning frameworks that place whiteness at the center and for finding new ways to tell the story of American religions.

© MADPHOTO.COM

CATHERINE L. ALBANESE is the J. F. Rowny Distinguished Professor Emerita in Comparative Religions at the University of California, Santa Barbara. A former president of the American Academy of Religion, she is the author of numerous books, including *A Republic of Mind and Spirit: A Cultural History of American Metaphysical Religion* (2007) and *The Delight Makers: Anglo-American Metaphysical Religion and the Pursuit of Happiness* (2023).

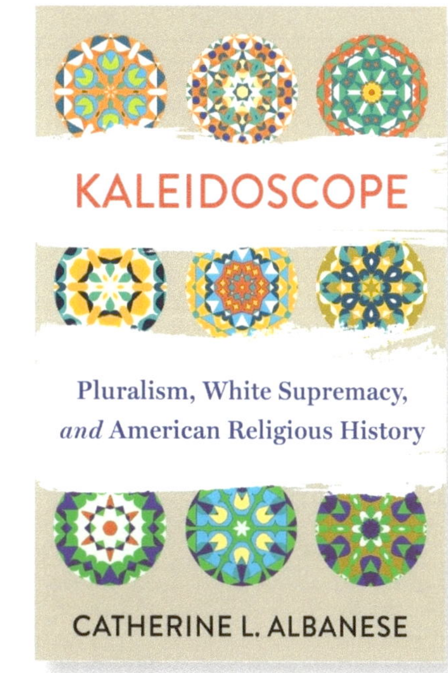

"Albanese's bracing book envisions America as a kaleidoscope that has failed many times and is failing today in this present of white supremacist politics. But Albanese dreams of a better future. The kaleidoscope turns again, and the present anti-Black, anti-immigrant, and anti-Semitic hatreds become possible breaking points, ways to wake up from the nightmare we are in. Not every American future is a dystopia. Neither is this one."

—Jeffrey J. Kripal, author of *How to Think Impossibly: About Souls, UFOs, Time, Belief, and Everything Else*

$30.00* / £25.00 paper 978-0-231-22354-6
$120.00 / £100.00 cloth 978-0-231-22353-9
JULY 248 pages / 5.5" x 8.5"
RELIGION
LECTURES ON THE HISTORY OF RELIGIONS

The Enigma of Gender

Why Identity Is Neither Individual Nor Essential

HANS-GEORG MOELLER

WHY DAOIST PHILOSOPHY OFFERS UNEXPECTED RESOURCES FOR UNDERSTANDING GENDER

Current debates about gender identity are fraught with contradictions. Even as we increasingly recognize gender as an assigned category or social convention, we still see it as inherent to who we are, fundamental to our sense of self. But the quest to find one's true self is unfulfillable. How can we find alternatives to the focus on getting our identity "right"?

This book offers a cultural critique of gender narratives, spanning traditional conformity to gender roles, the modern quest for individual authenticity beyond gender, and the recent social media–fueled concern with curating gendered profiles. Hans-Georg Moeller puts Daoist philosophy into conversation with present-day thinkers, showing why it helps us rethink common notions about identity. Discussing a wide range of cases, from Chinese foot binding to the politics around transgender issues today, he argues that we can defuse our anxieties by recognizing that gender—like all identities—is social, not individual, and changes at different times and in different places. Accessibly written and empathetic, *The Enigma of Gender* calls on us to be at ease with whoever we happen to be.

HANS-GEORG MOELLER is professor of philosophy at the University of Macau. His Columbia University Press books include *You and Your Profile: Identity After Authenticity* (2021) and *Genuine Pretending: On the Philosophy of the* Zhuangzi (2017), both with Paul J. D'Ambrosio.

The
Enigma of Gender
Why Identity
Is Neither Individual
Nor Essential

Hans-Georg Moeller

"Moeller's Daoist approach enriches contemporary debates regarding narratives about gender."

—Ellen Zhang, professor of comparative philosophy, University of Macau

"Through luminous insight and powerful clarity, Moeller opens a new horizon—gender ease, a Daoist way of being that flows beyond fixed categories and hardened identities."

—Robin R. Wang, author of *Yinyang: The Way of Heaven and Earth in Chinese Thought and Culture*

$27.00* / £22.00 paper 978-0-231-22128-3
$110.00 / £92.00 cloth 978-0-231-22127-6

FEBRUARY 232 pages / 5.5" x 8.5"

PHILOSOPHY

The Coffee Can Investor

A Stock-Picker's Journey to Build Generational Wealth

NEERAJ KHEMLANI

A GUIDE TO PICKING QUALITY STOCKS FOR THE VERY LONG HAUL

What would happen if you bought a handful of stocks and then left them alone for some time, like stashing valuables in a coffee can? If you picked the right ones, you might wake up one day with life-changing wealth.

Neeraj Khemlani introduces readers to this investing philosophy through the eye-opening story of a portfolio manager who has put it into practice. Matt Ankrum researched 100-baggers—stocks that have multiplied in value a hundred times over multiple decades—looking for what they have in common. Drawing on these clues, he hunts down and buys shares in what he thinks are tomorrow's breakout companies, planning to gift his children a coffee can portfolio that could someday be worth half a billion dollars.

The Coffee Can Investor shares Ankrum's process for identifying companies that can stand the test of time, as well as his stock picks. It explores the principles of long-term investing, emphasizing the power of compounding and why it pays to be patient. This book details the qualitative and quantitative aspects of 100-baggers, revealing that a surprising share are business-to-business companies, not just the business-to-consumer companies that typically grab headlines. Khemlani also recounts his own decision to make a coffee can of investments for his kids.

Engaging and fast-paced, this book is for anyone who wants to invest in enduring companies for the long term.

NEERAJ KHEMLANI is a veteran media executive and the former president and cohead of CBS News and Stations. He has also served in senior roles at Hearst and Yahoo! News and Finance, and has produced award-winning stories for *60 Minutes* and ABC News.

"*The Coffee Can Investor* is a gem of a book that combines good journalism with strong storytelling. It's an incredible story of two fathers' love for their children and their desire to leave them a future as big and bright as the Texas sky."

—Dan Rather, journalist and former national news anchor

$27.95t / £22.00 cloth 978-0-231-22106-1

MARCH 280 pages / 6.125" x 9.25" / 77 figures, 3 tables

BUSINESS / INVESTING

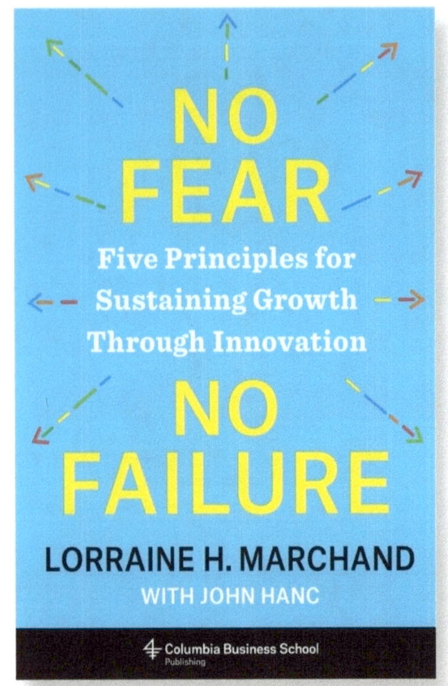

No Fear, No Failure

Five Principles for Sustaining Growth Through Innovation

LORRAINE H. MARCHAND WITH JOHN HANC

A GUIDE TO CREATING A BUSINESS CULTURE THAT WELCOMES INNOVATION AS A CORE VALUE

Many companies claim to prize innovation but struggle to support it in practice. CEOs call innovation their number-one priority in surveys, yet their employees say they are frequently frustrated in their efforts to create change. The biggest reason for this disconnect? Playing it safe. Leaders and organizations want to implement new ideas, but too often they are held back by the fear of failure, even though setbacks are intrinsic to the innovation process.

Lorraine H. Marchand shows readers how to overcome the status quo that stifles creative thinking and to create a culture that encourages innovation. She provides a framework for sustained growth built on the "5 Cs": Customer First, Culture, Collaboration, Change, and Chance. Drawing on more than 120 interviews with leaders across industries, real-world case studies, and firsthand experience, Marchand demonstrates how to spark lasting transformation. She shares field-tested strategies, tactics, and tools that practitioners can use to embed creativity within organizational cultures, leverage innovation to ensure better results, and future-proof a company for the long haul. Practical and inspiring, *No Fear, No Failure* is a step-by-step guide for organizations of every type and size to drive growth by fostering a culture of innovation.

LORRAINE H. MARCHAND is an acclaimed consultant, author, and educator on innovation with extensive experience in new product development. She has cofounded several start-ups; held leadership positions at companies including Bristol-Myers Squibb, Covance/LabCorp, and IBM; and served as advisor to Johnson & Johnson and Hewlett Packard. Marchand is the author of *The Innovation Mindset: Eight Essential Steps to Transform Any Industry* (Columbia, 2022). She teaches at the Wharton School of the University of Pennsylvania and Yeshiva University.

JOHN HANC is the author or coauthor of more than twenty books, as well as a longtime contributing writer to *Newsday*, the *New York Times*, and *Smithsonian*.

"A must-read for all leaders engaged in developing and nurturing new ideas into products and looking to make innovation a way of working and a lever for driving sustained growth."

—Nitesh Bansal, CEO, R-Systems; former president, Infosys

"Marchand shows us how to drive innovation into our way of working and thinking, helping us achieve sustained growth."

—David Valenzuela, national business director, Novartis Oncology, Rare Disease

$29.95t / £25.00 cloth 978-0-231-21920-4
FEBRUARY 304 pages / 5.5" x 8.5" / 5 b&w figures
BUSINESS / INNOVATION

Massively Better Healthcare

The Innovator's Guide to Tackling Healthcare's Biggest Challenges

HALLE TECCO

FIXING HEALTHCARE BY INNOVATING FROM THE INSIDE OUT

Healthcare is broken—but we can fix it. Our current system is plagued by staggering costs, inadequate outcomes, and pervasive inequities. How can we deliver long-overdue change and make this system work for everyone?

In this groundbreaking book, Halle Tecco provides an insider's guide to transforming our healthcare system through innovation. Drawing from her extensive experience as an entrepreneur, investor, and professor, she delivers a practical roadmap for addressing the most pressing challenges. Combining personal narratives, compelling case studies, and actionable frameworks, Tecco explores how to identify opportunities for meaningful change and build sustainable, scalable solutions that align profit with purpose. She acknowledges the difficulties—such as regulatory hurdles, misaligned incentives, and resistance to change—but shows how entrepreneurs can turn obstacles into their competitive advantage.

Bridging the gap between Silicon Valley dynamism and healthcare's evidence-based approach, *Massively Better Healthcare* offers a realistic yet optimistic view of what's possible. Written for everyone from seasoned professionals to aspiring innovators, this book shares an inspiring and attainable vision of a better healthcare system and equips readers with the essential tools to succeed.

HALLE TECCO is the founder of the venture fund Rock Health and an investor in more than fifty digital health companies. She is an adjunct professor at Columbia Business School and a course director at Harvard Medical School. She holds an MBA from Harvard Business School and an MPH from Johns Hopkins University.

Columbia Business School Publishing

"This book is a masterful exploration of how we can reimagine the delivery of healthcare. With real-world insights and compelling storytelling, Tecco doesn't just diagnose the problems: She provides a blueprint for meaningful, systemic change."

—Megan L. Ranney, dean of the Yale School of Public Health

"Tecco's roadmap equips the next generation of innovators with the insight they need to drive meaningful change."

—Aneesh Chopra, former chief technology officer of the United States

$32.00* / £28.00 cloth 978-0-231-22236-5

JANUARY 304 pages / 5.5" x 8.5" / 20 figures, 6 tables

HEALTH / INNOVATION

Columbia Business School Publishing

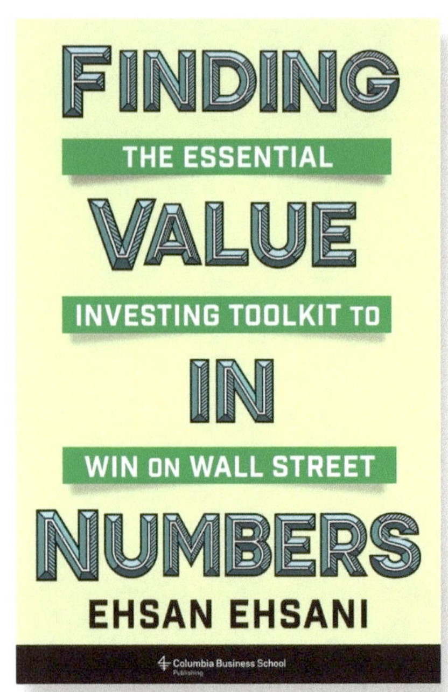

“What separates a good investor from a great one isn't genius—it's clarity of thought and a framework that withstands uncertainty. This book will arm curious MBA students and professional investors with quantitative tools and mental models to accomplish an analyst's most essential task: determining the gap between price and value. If you want to develop your own framework for security valuation, start here.”

—Bob Robotti, president and chief investment officer, Robotti & Company

Finding Value in Numbers

The Essential Investing Toolkit to Win on Wall Street

EHSAN EHSANI

Foreword by Mario Gabelli

AN INTRODUCTION TO MATHEMATICAL SKILLS AND QUANTITATIVE TOOLS FOR INVESTORS

To be successful as an investor, one needs a framework. And no investing framework works without numbers. Although quantitative methods can be intimidating, they provide a major boost to the quality of analysis. Written for readers without a technical background, *Finding Value in Numbers* is an engaging and practical guide to how thoughtful investors can use numbers—not just for the sake of crunching data but for making better decisions.

Using a value investing perspective, Ehsan Ehsani shows how to deploy quantitative tools to identify and analyze investment prospects, demystifying the math that points to overlooked opportunities in the stock market, other securities, and beyond. Numbers help us grasp what a company is worth and why: the quality of a business, the durability of its competitive edge, and the reasonableness of its price. Combining practical frameworks with real-world examples, Ehsani walks readers through key concepts that enable robust analysis while explaining how to spot red flags. Along the way, he reveals how a disciplined, numbers-based approach can support both conviction and patience—two traits every successful investor needs. Blending quantitative insight with timeless investing wisdom, *Finding Value in Numbers* is an essential book for aspiring and professional investors looking to hone their skills as well as curious readers drawn to the inner workings of markets.

EHSAN EHSANI is an adjunct professor in the finance division at Columbia Business School and an investor at an activist and value-oriented firm in New York. He holds an MBA from Columbia Business School, along with master's degrees from the MIT-Zaragoza International Logistics Program and Chalmers University of Technology in Sweden.

MARIO GABELLI is the chairman and chief executive officer of GAMCO Investors, Inc.

$30.00* / £25.00 cloth 978-0-231-21787-3

JANUARY 360 pages / 6.125" x 9.25" / 52 b&w figures, 89 tables

BUSINESS / INVESTING

HEILBRUNN CENTER FOR GRAHAM & DODD INVESTING SERIES

The Virtual Universe

Unlocking the Possibilities of the Metaverse

ANDREAS KAPLAN

A BUSINESS OVERVIEW OF THE PROSPECTS FOR THE METAVERSE

Will we one day inhabit virtual worlds? From the buzz around Second Life in the early 2000s to Mark Zuckerberg's much-hyped quest for the metaverse, there seems to be a clear pattern. After being touted as revolutionary, virtual worlds fail to meet expectations and fade into obscurity. Yet the dream of an immersive, independent, and interconnected virtual social universe still has the potential to transform the economy, reshape society, and profoundly affect the future of humanity.

This book contends that despite shifting trends, the virtual universe remains crucial to the technology of tomorrow—and might arrive sooner than we think. Through vivid examples and detailed case studies, Andreas Kaplan, a pioneering researcher of virtual worlds since the early 2000s, provides a comprehensive examination of the metaverse and its far-reaching implications. He delves into key technologies such as artificial intelligence, blockchain, and extended reality and discusses ethical issues around privacy, identity, and governance. Kaplan examines business models, digital ownership, and corporate strategies alongside applications spanning marketing, research and development, human resources, and supply chain management. The book concludes by contrasting potential futures, from utopian promise to dystopian peril and everything in between. Written in an engaging, reader-friendly style, *The Virtual Universe* goes beyond the hype—and the doubting—to uncover the true potential of the metaverse.

ANDREAS KAPLAN is professor of digital transformation and president of Kühne Logistics University and former dean of ESCP Business School, Sorbonne Alliance. An expert in AI, social media, and virtual reality, he has taught at Harvard University, Sciences Po Paris, and Tsinghua University. His books include *Artificial Intelligence, Business, and Civilization: Our Fate Made in Machines* (2022).

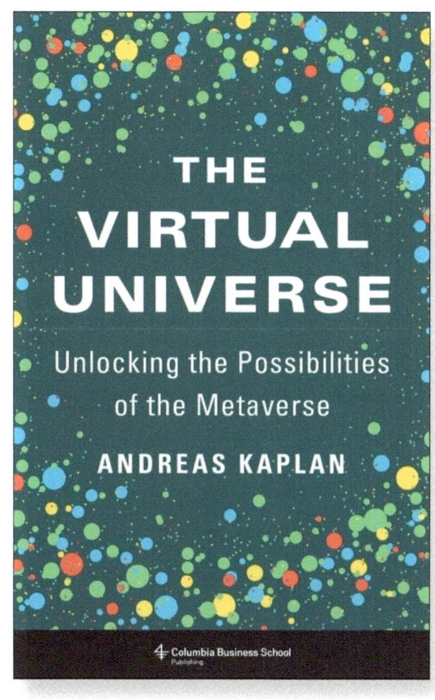

Columbia Business School Publishing

"*The Virtual Universe* offers a comprehensive overview of virtual reality, virtual worlds, and the future metaverse. Through an examination of the advantages and potential downsides, Kaplan presents a well-rounded and holistic perspective on the metaverse—an environment he aptly describes as a 'land of endless possibilities.'"

—Michael Haenlein, ESCP Business School and University of Liverpool Management School

$30.00* / £25.00 cloth 978-0-231-21768-2
MAY 248 pages / 5.5" x 8.5" / 6 figures, 6 tables
BUSINESS / TECHNOLOGY

Sustainability Metrics and Management

The Path from Innovation to Routine

STEVEN COHEN, WILLIAM EIMICKE, AND GUO DONG

HOW TO APPROACH THE BUSINESS IMPACTS OF SUSTAINABILITY

In recent years, increasingly sophisticated metrics have been created to measure sustainability. First devised to address environmental concerns such as greenhouse gas emissions, they now also assess organizational governance, community benefits, and hiring practices, among others. The field of sustainability management uses these metrics to track and advance progress on environmental, social, and business goals. How can an organization incorporate sustainability metrics into performance measurement and decision making? Which metrics should different organizations adopt, and why? What should sustainability management do to adapt in the face of political hostility, economic volatility, and technological change?

This is a comprehensive guide to sustainability metrics and management, introducing readers to key concepts and techniques. The authors show how to integrate sustainability into the core of organizational management and make it a routine part of administration. Written for practitioners, students, and managers of organizations of all sizes, this book gives readers the tools and understanding they need to lead the journey toward sustainability.

"Sustainability metrics are an essential part of any business transformation. The authors offer an insightful summary of the challenges of integrating sustainability into management practices for managers and emerging leaders alike. A wonderful book on an important topic."

—Peter McAteer, managing director, SustainLearning

STEVEN COHEN is senior vice dean of the School of Professional Studies, professor of practice in the School of International and Public Affairs, and director of the Earth Institute's Research Program on Sustainability Policy and Management as well as two other masters' programs at Columbia University.

WILLIAM B. EIMICKE is professor of practice and founding director of the Picker Center for Executive Education at Columbia University's School of International and Public Affairs. He was previously New York City's deputy fire commissioner and New York State's housing "czar."

GUO DONG is professor of practice in sustainability management and associate director of the Research Program on Sustainability Policy and Management at Columbia University.

$28.00* / £22.00 paper 978-0-231-22067-5
$110.00 / £92.00 cloth 978-0-231-22066-8
APRIL 232 pages / 5.5" x 8.5" / 2 b&w figures
MANAGEMENT / SUSTAINABILITY

Making Organizational Culture Great

Moving Beyond Popular Beliefs

JENNIFER A. CHATMAN AND GLENN R. CARROLL

A GUIDE TO LEVERAGING ORGANIZATIONAL CULTURE FOR STRATEGIC SUCCESS

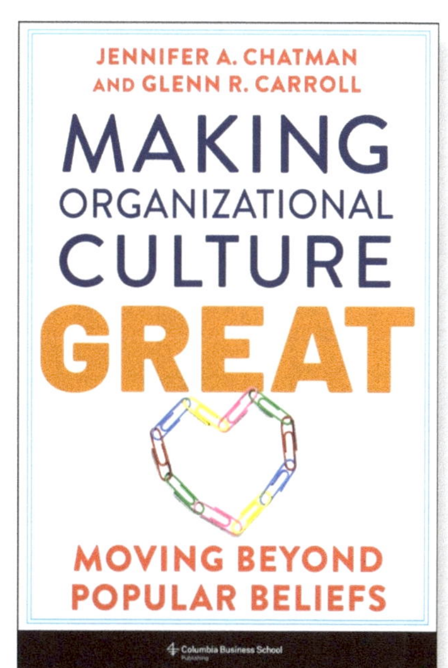

Columbia Business School Publishing

Leaders remain skeptical about the power of organizational culture even though extensive research shows that it is crucial to business success. Can a manager really influence an organization's culture, or do executives just try to impose a culture on their employees? Is the concept of culture too vague to measure objectively? What happens to valuable employees who feel left out? Even if culture makes team members happy, does it actually affect the bottom line?

This essential book answers the biggest questions about organizational culture, offering research-backed insights for leaders on shaping and managing an environment that spurs achievement. The management experts Jennifer A. Chatman and Glenn R. Carroll—a psychologist and a sociologist—draw on social-scientific findings to evaluate and debunk common misconceptions. They show how research on culture empowers managers to identify what really matters and deploy it productively.

Making Organizational Culture Great features compelling examples from companies and nonprofits including Apple, Genentech, Disney, Ford, Netflix, Maersk, Google, Cisco, Southwest Airlines, and many others. A practical guide for current and aspiring leaders, this book reveals how to manage culture consistently, comprehensively, and coherently.

JENNIFER A. CHATMAN is Bank of America Dean of the Haas School of Business at the University of California, Berkeley, and codirector of the Berkeley Haas Center for Workplace Culture and Innovation. She is cohost of the podcast *The Culture Kit with Jenny and Sameer*.

GLENN R. CARROLL is Adams Distinguished Professor of Management at the Stanford Graduate School of Business and professor (by courtesy) of sociology at Stanford University. He is coauthor of *Making Great Strategy: Arguing for Organizational Advantage* (Columbia, 2021).

"Chatman and Carroll provide leaders with pragmatic and robust practices for aligning culture and strategy. This is the book for managers interested in lifting their organization to new heights!"

—Kristin Sverchek, former president, Lyft

"This book busts some of the biggest myths about organizational culture. With rigorous evidence and vivid cases, two experts illuminate how to understand and improve systems of values, norms, and behaviors."

—Adam Grant, *New York Times* bestselling author of *Hidden Potential* and *Think Again* and host of the podcast *Re:Thinking*

$24.95t / £20.00 paper 978-0-231-22136-8
$100.00 / £84.00 cloth 978-0-231-22137-5

APRIL 304 pages / 5.5" x 8.5" / 41 b&w figures, 5 tables

BUSINESS / MANAGEMENT

Julia Kristeva is among the world's most acclaimed and accomplished thinkers. Born in Bulgaria in 1941, she has lived and worked in France since 1966, becoming one of the country's most important public intellectuals. A renowned psychoanalyst, philosopher, and linguist, she has written dozens of books spanning semiotics, political theory, literary criticism, gender and sex, and cultural critique, as well as several novels and autobiographical works, that have been influential worldwide. Kristeva is professor emerita of linguistics at the Université de Paris VII. She was the inaugural recipient of the Holberg International Memorial Prize in 2004 "for innovative explorations of questions on the intersection of language, culture, and literature."

Columbia University Press is proud to have been the publisher of Kristeva's books in English translation for more than four decades, helping her vital body of work reach a global readership. This season, we continue the Kristeva Library, reissuing her works with a bold new look and a unified format, with striking new covers and updated interior design to ensure that these essential books continue to inspire and provoke readers around the world for years to come. Last season, we brought you *Teresa, My Love*; *Murder in Byzantium*; *The Enchanted Clock*; *Dostoyevsky, or the Flood of Language*; and *Proust and the Sense of Time* and this catalog features three more of her major works.

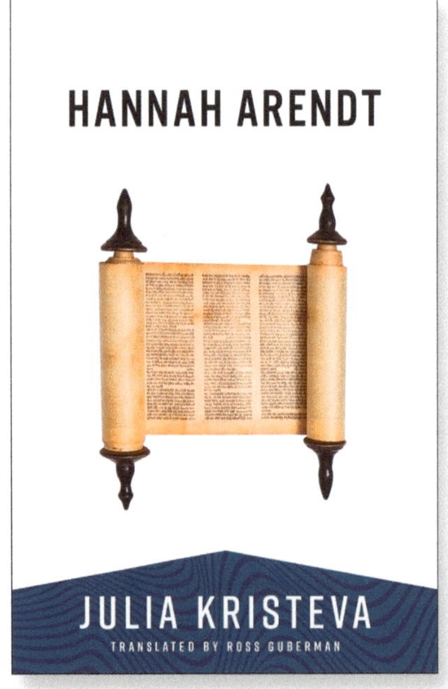

"Traces [Arendt's life and thought] rigorously and with strong interpretive opinions."

—*Publishers Weekly*

$25.00* / £20.00 paper 978-0-231-22393-5

JUNE 320 pages / 5.5" x 8.5" / 4 images

PHILOSOPHY

EUROPEAN PERSPECTIVES: A SERIES IN SOCIAL THOUGHT AND CULTURAL CRITICISM

World English-language Rights: Columbia University Press; All Other Rights: Librairie Arthème Fayard

Hannah Arendt

JULIA KRISTEVA

Translated by Ross Guberman

We are still coming to terms with the controversial figure of Hannah Arendt (1906–1975). Interlacing her life and work, this book is an elegant, sophisticated biography brimming with historical and philosophical insight. Focusing on the theme of female genius, Julia Kristeva emphasizes three features of the philosopher's work. Exploring Arendt's critique of Saint Augustine and her biographical essay on Rahel Varnhagen, Kristeva accentuates Arendt's commitment to recounting lives. Second, she reflects on Arendt's perspective on Judaism, anti-Semitism, and the "banality of evil." Finally, Kristeva assesses Arendt's intellectual journey, placing her enthusiasm for observing both social phenomena and political events in the context of her personal life. Drawing on fragments of Arendt's correspondence with her longtime lover Martin Heidegger and her husband Heinrich Blucher, excerpts from her mother's diary, and passages from Arendt's philosophical writings, this book presents a luminous account of an essential thinker.

ROSS GUBERMAN translated several works by Julia Kristeva, including *New Maladies of the Soul* and *Time and Sense: Proust and the Experience of Literature*.

Melanie Klein

JULIA KRISTEVA

Translated by Ross Guberman

"Kristeva, a formidable cultural historian and critic, brings a rich mix of data and ideas."

—*Library Journal*

Melanie Klein (1882–1960) pioneered psychoanalytic practice with children and introduced a new approach to the theory of the unconscious. In her first biography of a fellow psychoanalyst, Julia Kristeva tells the remarkable story of Klein's life: an unhappy wife and mother who underwent analysis and—without a medical or other advanced degree—became an analyst herself at the age of forty. In Kristeva's account, Klein was the first person to see the mother as the source of not only creativity but also thought as well as the first to consider the place of matricide in psychic development—making her a crucial figure in the evolution of the provocative ideas about motherhood and the psyche for which Kristeva is renowned.

ROSS GUBERMAN translated several works by Julia Kristeva, including *New Maladies of the Soul* and *Time and Sense: Proust and the Experience of Literature*.

$25.00* / £20.00 paper 978-0-231-22392-8

JUNE 304 pages / 5.5" x 8.5"

PHILOSOPHY / PSYCHOLOGY

EUROPEAN PERSPECTIVES: A SERIES IN SOCIAL THOUGHT AND CULTURAL CRITICISM

World English-language Rights: Columbia University Press; All Other Rights: Librairie Arthème Fayard

Colette

JULIA KRISTEVA

Translated by Jane Marie Todd

"Persuasive and entertaining. . . . Kristeva and Colette are a brilliant coupling."

—*The Times (UK)*

The final volume of Julia Kristeva's trilogy on "female genius," *Colette* interlaces commentary on the life and work of the notorious French author who made it possible for women to write erotic literature. Colette (1873–1954) was a prolific novelist who celebrated sexual pleasure at a time when women writers were inhibited about dealing with the topic. She also published in pro-Vichy, anti-Semitic journals during the Nazi occupation, even as she fought to keep her Jewish third husband from deportation. Kristeva offers an elegant and sophisticated critique of Colette's psychological conflicts, opening Colette's oeuvre to psychoanalytic interpretation.

JANE MARIE TODD (1957–2021) translated more than ninety books for university presses and art museums.

$25.00 / £20.00 paper 978-0-231-22391-1

JUNE 448 pages / 5.5" x 8.5" / 10 images

PHILOSOPHY / LITERARY STUDIES

EUROPEAN PERSPECTIVES: A SERIES IN SOCIAL THOUGHT AND CULTURAL CRITICISM

World English-language Rights: Columbia University Press; All Other Rights: Librairie Arthème Fayard

NEW IN PAPER

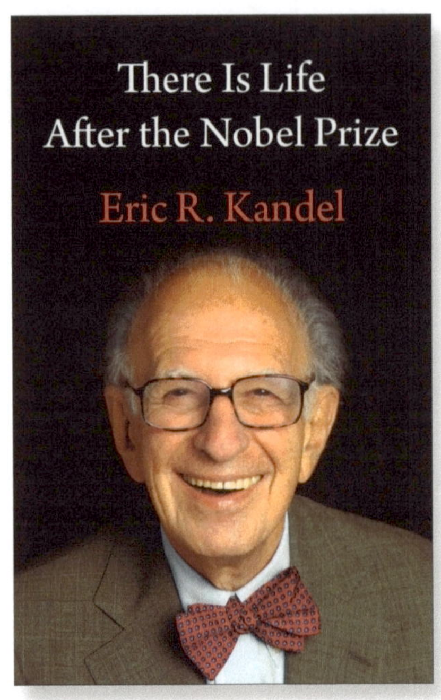

"In this remarkable recap of his post-prize career, Kandel's intellect and passion are present on every page. Readers will be awed by the depth and breadth of Kandel's work."

—*Publishers Weekly*

"A short, cheerful memoir from an energetic Nobel laureate."

—*Kirkus*

There Is Life After the Nobel Prize

ERIC R. KANDEL

One day in 1996, the neuroscientist Eric R. Kandel took a call from his program officer at the National Institute of Mental Health, who informed him that he had been awarded a key grant. Also, the officer said, he and his colleagues thought Kandel would win the Nobel Prize. "I hope not soon," Kandel's wife, Denise, said when she heard this. Sociologists had found that Nobel Prize winners often did not contribute much more to science, she explained.

In this book, Kandel recounts his remarkable career since receiving the Nobel in 2000—or his experience of proving to his wife that he was not yet "completely dead intellectually." He takes readers through his lab's scientific advances, including research into how long-term memory is stored in the brain, the nature of age-related memory loss, and the neuroscience of drug addiction and schizophrenia. Kandel relates how the Nobel Prize gave him the opportunity to reach a far larger audience, which in turn allowed him to discover and pursue new directions. He describes his efforts to promote public understanding of science and to put brain science and art into conversation with each other. Kandel also discusses his return to Austria, which he had fled as a child, and observes Austria's coming to terms with the Nazi period. Showcasing Kandel's accomplishments, erudition, and wit, *There Is Life After the Nobel Prize* is a candid account of the working life of an acclaimed scientist.

ERIC R. KANDEL is University Professor Emeritus at Columbia University. He is founding codirector of Columbia University's Zuckerman Institute, founding director of Columbia's Kavli Institute for Brain Science, and Sagol Professor Emeritus of Brain Science at the Zuckerman Institute. In 2000 he was awarded the Nobel Prize in Physiology or Medicine for his studies of learning and memory. He is the author of *In Search of Memory: The Emergence of a New Science of Mind* (2006); *The Age of Insight: The Quest to Understand the Unconscious in Art, Mind, and Brain, from Vienna 1900 to the Present* (2012); *Reductionism in Art and Brain Science: Bridging the Two Cultures* (Columbia, 2016); *The Disordered Mind: What Unusual Brains Tell Us About Ourselves* (2018); and *Essays on Art and Science* (Columbia, 2024).

$17.00* / £13.99 paper 978-0-231-22420-8

JUNE 120 pages / 5.06" x 7.81" / 11 figures

SCIENCE

CLOTH EDITION 2021 978-0-231-20014-1

World English-language Rights: Columbia University Press; All Other Rights: The Wylie Agency

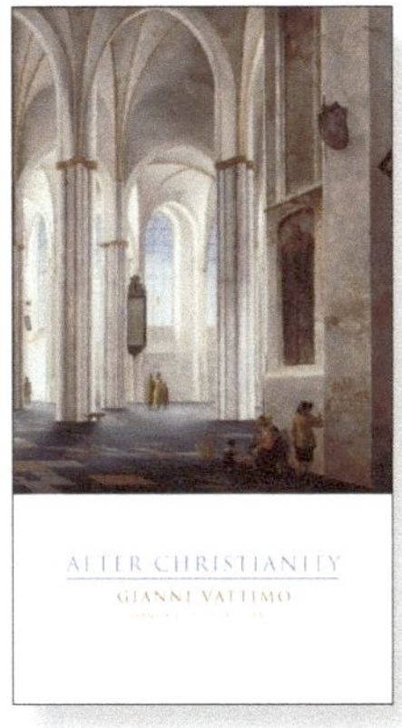

After Christianity

GIANNI VATTIMO

Translated by Luca D'Isanto

"In this remarkable book, Vattimo engages in an unyielding analysis of the state of life in the West after Christianity."

—*Journal of Religion*

What has been the fate of Christianity since Nietzsche's famous announcement of the "death of God"? Gianni Vattimo offers a brilliant examination of Christianity in an age of deep uncertainty—and a personal account of how he himself recovered his faith through Nietzsche and Heidegger.

GIANNI VATTIMO (1936–2023) was emeritus professor of philosophy at the University of Turin and a former member of the European Parliament. His Columbia University Press books include *Of Reality: The Purposes of Philosophy* (2016) and *A Farewell to Truth* (2011).

LUCA D'ISANTO has translated works including Vattimo's *Art's Claim to Truth* (Columbia, 2008).

$20.00* / £16.99 paper 978-0-231-22387-4
JANUARY 128 pages / 5.1" x 9.1"
PHILOSOPHY
CLOTH EDITION 2002 978-0-231-10628-3
ITALIAN ACADEMY LECTURES

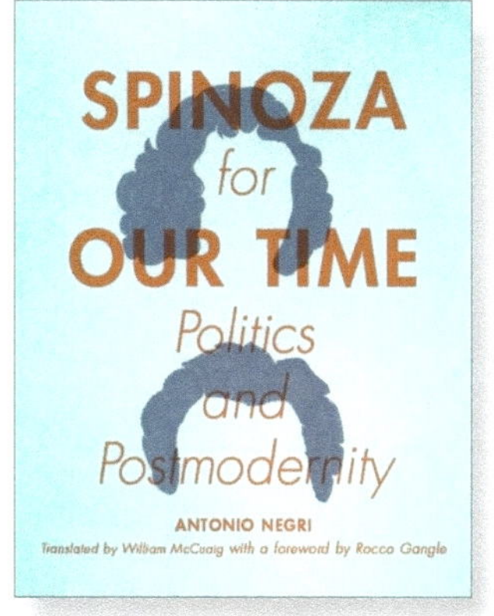

Spinoza for Our Time

Politics and Postmodernity

ANTONIO NEGRI

Translated by William McCuaig

With a foreword by Rocco Gangle

"Piercingly insightful."

—*The Comparatist*

Antonio Negri offers a profound understanding of Baruch Spinoza and his legacy, demonstrating the thinker's ongoing relevance. By positioning Spinoza as a revolutionary intellectual, Negri advances his philosophy of the multitude, immanence, and political action.

ANTONIO NEGRI (1933–2023) was a world-renowned theorist who taught political philosophy at the University of Padua, the University of Vincennes, and College Internationale de Philosophie. His books include *Factory of Strategy: Thirty-Three Lessons on Lenin* (Columbia, 2014). With Michael Hardt, he coauthored the best-selling trilogy, *Empire*, *Multitude*, and *Commonwealth*.

WILLIAM McCUAIG is the translator of many books by Gianni Vattimo, including *A Farewell to Truth* (Columbia, 2011).

ROCCO GANGLE is associate professor of philosophy at Endicott College.

$20.00* / £16.99 paper 978-0-231-22419-2
JANUARY 152 pages / 5.5" x 7"
PHILOSOPHY
CLOTH EDITION 2013 978-0-231-16046-9
INSURRECTIONS: CRITICAL STUDIES IN RELIGION, POLITICS, AND CULTURE

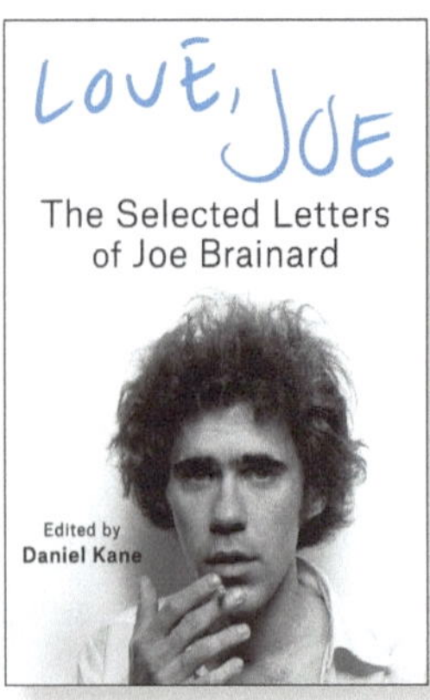

Love, Joe

The Selected Letters of Joe Brainard

JOE BRAINARD

Edited by Daniel Kane

"In these letters, you feel the force of a person fully met."

—New York Times Book Review

Love, Joe presents a selection of Joe Brainard's letters stretching from 1959 to 1993, offering an intimate view of his personal and artistic life. Brainard's letters to his partner, Kenward Elmslie, and others also open a window onto the transformations of queer life during this period.

"Offers glimpses of [Brainard's] constant play and productivity."

—New Yorker

JOE BRAINARD (1942–1994) was raised in Tulsa, Oklahoma, and moved to New York City in 1960. His *I Remember* has been translated into fifteen languages, and his artworks are in the collections of the Metropolitan Museum of Art, the Museum of Modern Art, the Whitney Museum, and many others. He died from AIDS-related pneumonia.

DANIEL KANE is a professor of American literature at Uppsala University. His books include *"Do You Have a Band?": Poetry and Punk Rock in New York City* (Columbia, 2017).

$27.00* / £22.00 paper 978-0-231-22388-1

MAY 408 pages / 6.125" x 9.25" / 33 b&w scans of letters/sketches

POETRY / ART / LETTERS

CLOTH EDITION 2024 978-0-231-20342-5

Black Intellectuals and Black Society

MARTIN L. KILSON

Foreword by Cornel West

"Kilson was the consummate teacher, and in this posthumous work of wide-ranging thought and scholarship, he brilliantly explores the pivotal yet often obscured legacy of giants of the twentieth-century African American intelligentsia."

—Henry Louis Gates, Jr., Alphonse Fletcher University Professor, Harvard University

This book presents the trailblazing political scientist Martin L. Kilson's essays on leading Black intellectuals of the twentieth century. Kilson argues that the trajectory of twentieth-century Black intellectuals was determined by the interplay between formal ideas and Black egalitarian struggle.

MARTIN L. KILSON (1931–2019) was Frank G. Thomson Professor of Government Emeritus at Harvard University. He wrote and edited several books, including *Transformation of the African American Intelligentsia, 1880–2012* (2014) and *A Black Intellectual's Odyssey: From a Pennsylvania Milltown to the Ivy League* (2021). He was a fellow of the American Academy of Arts and Sciences, a Guggenheim Fellow, a member of the National Endowment for the Humanities, and a longtime member of the editorial board of *Dissent*.

CORNEL WEST is the Dietrich Bonhoeffer Chair at Union Theological Seminary.

$26.00 / £22.00 paper 978-0-231-22390-4

JANUARY 296 pages / 6" x 9"

HISTORY / BLACK STUDIES

CLOTH EDITION 2024 978-0-231-21565-7

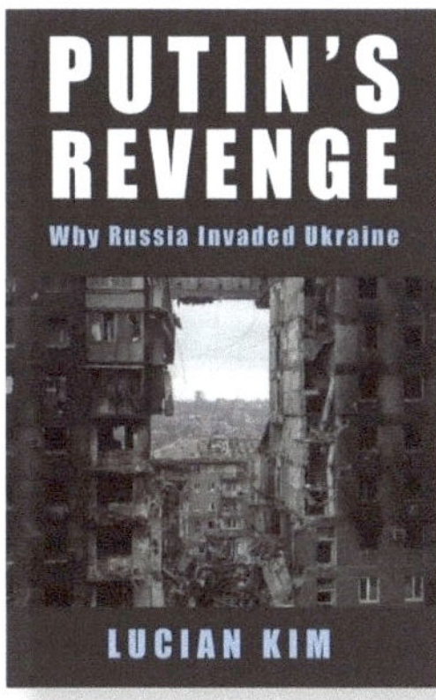

Putin's Revenge

Why Russia Invaded Ukraine

LUCIAN KIM

"Kim draws on his decades of pioneering and revelatory reporting to guide us through the twists and turns leading to Vladimir Putin's invasion of Ukraine. This is *the* book for anyone who wants to understand exactly why and how Putin launched Europe's largest land war since WWII."

—Fiona Hill, The Brookings Institution

Lucian Kim offers a gripping, definitive account of Russia's path to war, from Ukraine's 2004 Orange Revolution and the 2014 Maidan uprising right up to the full-scale invasion. He examines the Kremlin's motives, tracing Putin's transformation from a seemingly pragmatic leader into an embittered tyrant who saw it as his historical mission to reconquer Ukraine. This book tells the story of the lead-up to the invasion with revelatory detail and fresh analysis, shedding new light on a conflict that has roiled the post–Cold War order.

LUCIAN KIM has reported on Ukraine and Russia since Vladimir Putin's first term in office. Based in Moscow and Berlin for more than twenty years, he covered central and eastern Europe as a correspondent for National Public Radio, Bloomberg News, and the *Christian Science Monitor*.

$23.00* / £18.99 paper 978-0-231-22389-8

FEBRUARY 344 pages / 6" x 9" / 6 b&w maps

POLITICS

CLOTH EDITION 2024 978-0-231-21402-5

WOODROW WILSON CENTER SERIES

All Rights: Columbia University Press

Defeating Dengue

A Multistakeholder Approach to Problem Solving

R. EDWARD FREEMAN AND ANDREW SELL

FINALIST, 2025 SIM OUTSTANDING BOOK AWARD, SOCIAL ISSUES IN MANAGEMENT DIVISION, ACADEMY OF MANAGEMENT

This book tells the remarkable story of how a multistakeholder partnership in Indonesia fought dengue fever and explores the implications for social enterprises seeking to tackle the world's biggest challenges. It is at once an insightful case study of the power of multistakeholder partnerships and a gripping story of scientific and social achievement.

R. EDWARD FREEMAN is University Professor, Elis and Signe Olsson Professor of Business Administration, and academic director of the Institute for Business in Society at the University of Virginia Darden School of Business. He is the author of the influential *Strategic Management: A Stakeholder Approach* (2010, originally published in 1984) and coauthor of *The Power of And: Responsible Business Without Trade-Offs* (Columbia, 2020), among other books.

ANDREW SELL is a senior research associate with the Virginia Department of Social Services. He was previously senior associate director of research at the University of Virginia's Darden School of Business.

$22.00 / £17.99 paper 978-0-231-22418-5

APRIL 224 pages / 5.5" x 8.5" / 15 images

BUSINESS

CLOTH EDITION 2024 978-0-231-21556-5

All Rights: Columbia University Press

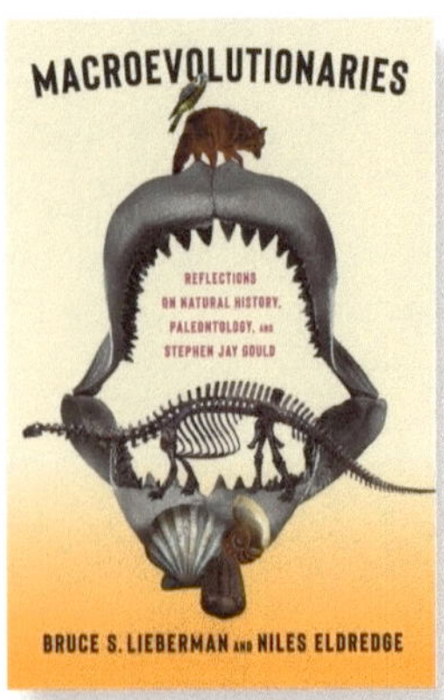

Macroevolutionaries

Reflections on Natural History, Paleontology, and Stephen Jay Gould

BRUCE S. LIEBERMAN AND NILES ELDREDGE

"[An] impressive book by impressive people. At once thought-provoking and entertaining."

—Jodi Summers, Southern California Paleontology Society

One of the twentieth century's great paleontologists and science writers, Stephen Jay Gould was, for Bruce S. Lieberman and Niles Eldredge, also a close colleague and friend. In *Macroevolutionaries*, they take up the tradition of Gould's acclaimed essays on natural history, offering a series of wry and insightful reflections on the fields to which they have devoted their careers.

BRUCE S. LIEBERMAN is Dean's Professor of Evolutionary Biology and senior curator of invertebrate paleontology at the University of Kansas, where he also directs the Paleontological Institute and is editor in chief of the *Treatise on Invertebrate Paleontology*.

NILES ELDREDGE is an invertebrate paleontologist, an evolutionary biologist, and an emeritus curator of invertebrates at the American Museum of Natural History. He discovered punctuated equilibria with Stephen Jay Gould and played a leading role in developing the field of macroevolution.

$22.00 / £17.99 paper 978-0-231-22416-1
APRIL 224 pages / 6.125" x 9.25" / 43 images
SCIENCE
CLOTH EDITION 2024 978-0-231-20810-9
All Rights: Columbia University Press

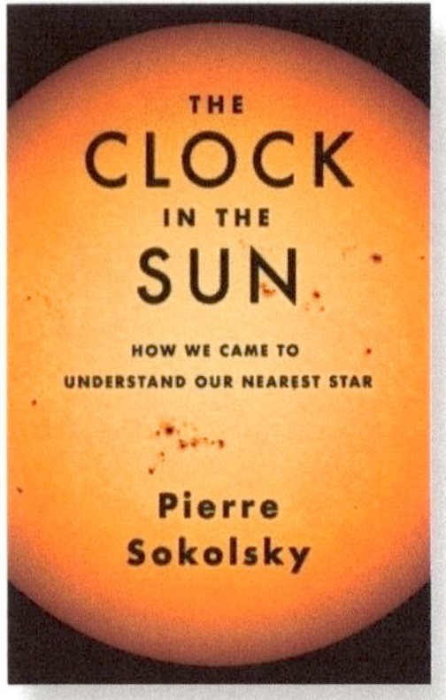

The Clock in the Sun

How We Came to Understand Our Nearest Star

PIERRE SOKOLSKY

"Provides a unique look at world history as seen through the lens of solar astronomy."

—*Wall Street Journal*

Pierre Sokolsky offers a history of knowledge of the Sun through the lens of sunspots and the solar cycle. He ranges widely across cultures and throughout history, from the earliest recorded observations of sunspots in Chinese annals to satellites orbiting the Sun today. Considering how various thinkers sought to solve the puzzle of sunspots, Sokolsky sheds new light on key discoveries and the people who made them, as well as their historical and cultural contexts.

PIERRE SOKOLSKY is distinguished professor of physics and astronomy emeritus at the University of Utah, where he was also dean of the College of Science. Sokolsky is a recipient of the American Physical Society's Panofsky Prize in High Energy Physics and the International Union of Pure and Applied Physics Yodh Prize.

"Interested readers of all levels will have something to learn and enjoy."

—*Open Letters Review*

$26.00 / £22.00 paper 978-0-231-22417-8
MAY 336 pages / 5.5" x 8.5" / 34 images
SCIENCE
CLOTH EDITION 2024 978-0-231-20248-0
All Rights: Columbia University Press

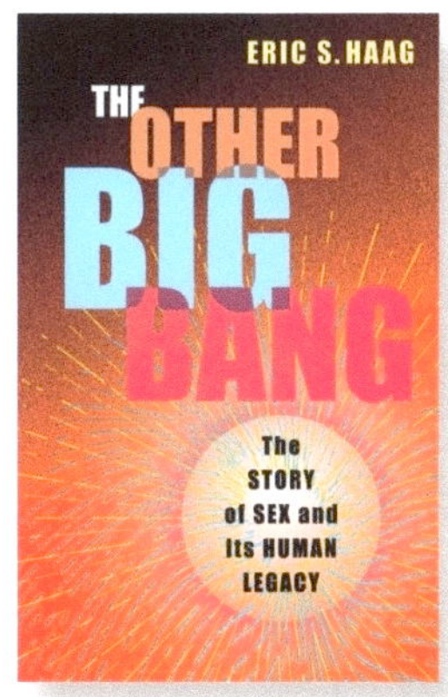

The Other Big Bang

The Story of Sex and Its Human Legacy

ERIC S. HAAG

"Engaging. . . . Excellent discussion material. Highly recommended."

—*Choice Reviews*

Eric S. Haag explores the two-billion-year history of sex, from the first organisms on Earth to contemporary humans. He delves into the deep history of sexual reproduction, from its origins as a fix for a mutational crisis to an essential feature of all complex life. Haag traces sexual differentiation from its earliest forms in microbes to its elaboration in animals, showing why sex differences in cells and organisms help species adapt, persist, and evolve. Bringing the story up to the present, Haag argues that the evolutionary history of human sexuality helps us better understand contemporary society.

ERIC S. HAAG is professor of biology and director of the Biological Sciences Graduate Program at the University of Maryland, College Park. He has conducted research on the evolution of sex and reproduction in animals such as sea urchins, roundworms, and hermaphroditic fish for three decades.

$26.00* / £22.00 paper 978-0-231-22415-4

MARCH 304 pages / 6.125" x 9.25" / 42 figures

SCIENCE

CLOTH EDITION 2024 978-0-231-20714-0

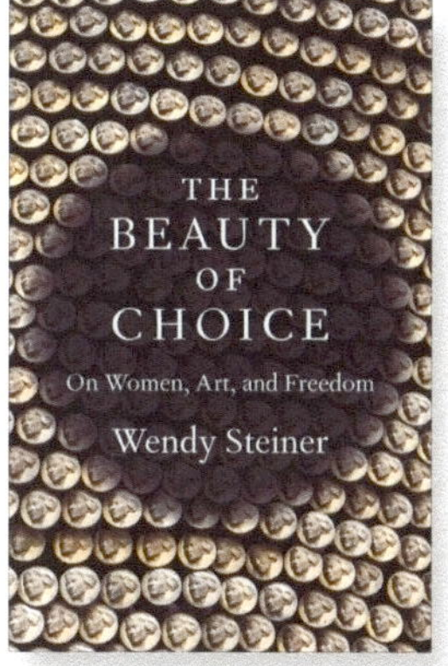

The Beauty of Choice

On Women, Art, and Freedom

WENDY STEINER

"A wildly inventive mix of erudition and insight, research and storytelling, a gorgeous and impassioned call to arms written in prose as clear as an alpine lake. Read this book and marvel."

—Andrea Barnet, author of *Visionary Women: How Rachel Carson, Jane Jacobs, Jane Goodall, and Alice Waters Changed Our World*

In *The Beauty of Choice*, the renowned cultural critic Wendy Steiner offers a dazzling new account of aesthetics grounded in female agency. Through a series of linked meditations on canonical and contemporary literature and art, she casts women's taste as the engine of liberal values. This deeply original book gives taste, beauty, and pleasure central roles in a passionate defense of women's freedom.

WENDY STEINER is Richard L. Fisher Professor of English Emerita at the University of Pennsylvania as well as an opera librettist and multimedia artist. Her many acclaimed books include *The Scandal of Pleasure: Art in an Age of Fundamentalism* (1995) and *Venus in Exile: The Rejection of Beauty in Twentieth-Century Art* (2001).

$26.00 / £22.00 paper 978-0-231-22400-0

MAY 288 pages / 5.5" x 8.5" / 55 b&w illustrations; 8 color images

PHILOSOPHY

CLOTH EDITION 2024 978-0-231-21526-8

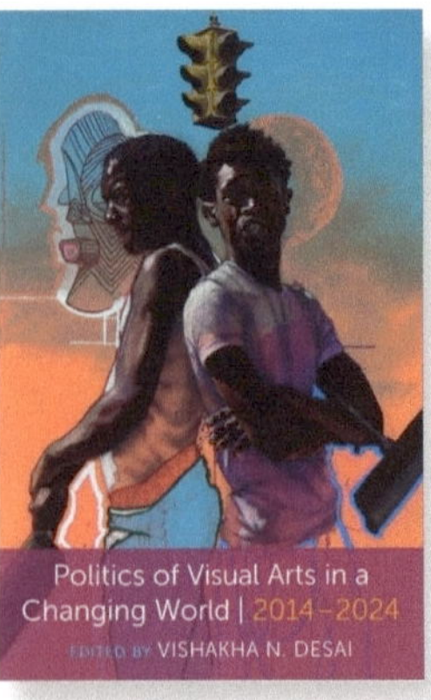

Politics of Visual Arts in a Changing World

2014–2024

VISHAKHA N. DESAI, EDITOR

"A vital collection that reveals how art and museums around the world are reckoning with some of the most urgent issues of our time—race, gender, class, and colonialism. Desai has curated an expansive conversation that is both global and profoundly grounded in lived institutional experience."

—Carol Becker, professor and dean emerita, Columbia University School of the Arts

Bringing together artists, scholars, activists, and museum professionals from varied fields and backgrounds, this book explores the intersections between visual art and social movements during the last tumultuous decade. Spanning themes of protest art, museum ethics, restitution, and institutional transformation, the collection considers how visual arts have both responded to and shaped politics and society.

VISHAKHA N. DESAI is an internationally recognized scholar, educator, and museum leader. She has been a senior advisor to President Lee C. Bollinger and chair of the Committee on Global Thought at Columbia University, and she is the past president and CEO of Asia Society. Her books include *World as Family: A Journey of Multi-Rooted Belongings* (Columbia, 2021).

$45.00 / £35.00 paper 978-0-231-21562-6
$180.00 / £140.00 cloth 978-0-231-21561-9
MAY 560 pages / 6.125" x 9.25" / 133 b&w images and 15 color images
ART

RELIGION

Dogs Save

Stories of Canine Redemption in US Culture

KATHARINE MERSHON

"An urgent, necessary read for those seeking to understand our enduring intimacy with animals—a sacred bond that Mershon fearlessly examines."

—Colin Dayan, author of *With Dogs at the Edge of Life*

Stories about people and dogs saving one another are everywhere in US culture—on TV, in Hollywood movies, on social media, and even on bumper stickers. Katharine Mershon examines the unacknowledged religious underpinnings of stories about dogs, revealing deeply rooted cultural assumptions about who can be saved and how redemption ought to occur. *Dogs Save* considers examples including the Michael Vick dogfighting case; Samuel Fuller's controversial B-movie *White Dog*; the TV show *The Dog Whisperer*; Laurie Anderson's film *Heart of a Dog*; and Eileen Myles's *Afterglow (a dog memoir)*.

KATHARINE MERSHON is assistant professor of philosophy and religion at Western Carolina University.

$30.00 / £25.00 paper 978-0-231-20697-6
$120.00 / £94.00 cloth 978-0-231-20696-9
APRIL 240 pages / 5.5" x 8.5" / 9 b&w film stills
RELIGION / ANIMAL STUDIES
CRITICAL PERSPECTIVES ON ANIMALS: THEORY, CULTURE, SCIENCE, AND LAW

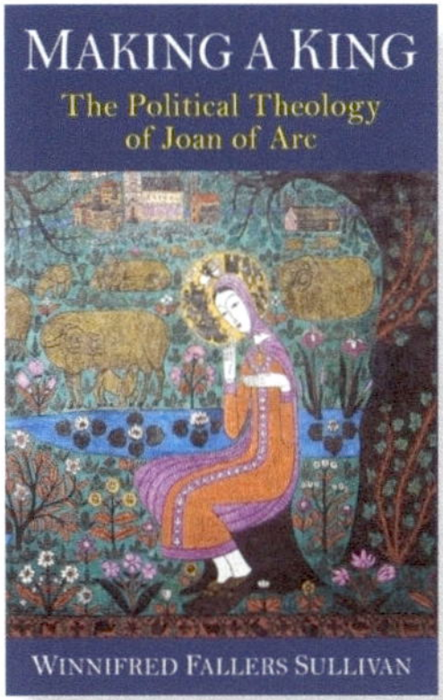

Making a King

The Political Theology of Joan of Arc

WINNIFRED FALLERS SULLIVAN

"This book is political theology at its very best."

—Vincent W. Lloyd, coauthor of *What Is Political Theology?*

There is an enduring fascination with Joan of Arc, yet she is almost always seen alone, as a victim or martyr. Focusing on her life rather than her death, Winnifred Fallers Sullivan offers an interpretation of Joan as a political thinker and actor who sought, during her meteoric presence in fifteenth-century France, to legitimate a king, channel God's word, convene a coronation, and speak for the people in an alternative legal order. *Making a King* illuminates Joan's extraordinary life and vision—her conception of sovereignty from below, her form of female masculinity, and her power as kingmaker—and shows why she can help us find a deeper understanding of religion and politics today.

WINNIFRED FALLERS SULLIVAN is Provost Professor Emeritus at Indiana University Bloomington, where she was the founding director of the Center for Religion and the Human. Her books include *The Impossibility of Religious Freedom* (2005) and *Church State Corporation: Construing Religion in US Law* (2020).

$32.00 / £28.00 paper 978-0-231-22282-2
$130.00 / £109.00 cloth 978-0-231-22281-5

JUNE 296 pages / 5.5" x 8.5" / 11 b&w illustrations

RELIGION

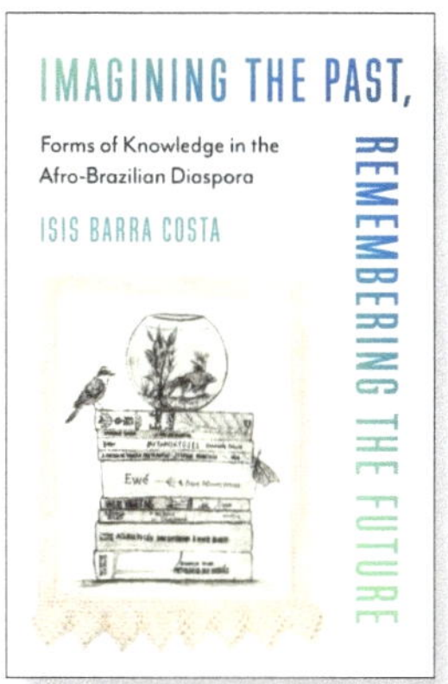

Imagining the Past, Remembering the Future

Forms of Knowledge in the Afro-Brazilian Diaspora

ISIS BARRA COSTA

"Beautiful and necessary."

—Zeca Ligiéro, artist and dean of the Center for Letters and Arts, Federal University of the State of Rio de Janeiro

Imagining the Past, Remembering the Future investigates the interlinked art, history, religion, philosophy, and cosmology of oral traditions across the Afro-Brazilian diaspora. Through case studies of sacred and secular performances, Isis Barra Costa shows how Afro-Brazilian concepts and practices preserve and renew an ever-changing diasporic philosophy. Ranging across parades of Black royal courts, Carnaval performing groups, oracular literature, "spirit-dictated" novels, and many other forms, she illuminates the survival and transformation of African cosmologies, epistemologies, and poetics in the Americas.

ISIS BARRA COSTA is assistant professor of contemporary Brazilian cultural and literary studies at the Ohio State University.

$40.00 / £30.00 paper 978-0-231-21263-2
$160.00 / £125.00 cloth 978-0-231-21262-5

FEBRUARY 424 pages / 6.125" x 9.25"

RELIGION

BLACK LIVES IN THE DIASPORA: PAST / PRESENT / FUTURE

Local Gods

A Philosophy of Spiritual Diversity

LEAH KALMANSON

"A magnificent book, staggering in scope and humbling in depth. It's been a while since I've been so excited about the philosophy of religion."

—Mary-Jane Rubenstein, author of *Pantheologies: Gods, Worlds, Monsters*

In many places around the world, spiritual matters and practices are local and contextual. Yet philosophy of religion often takes universalizing monotheism as the norm and overlooks other traditions, which it categorizes with oversimplified terms such as polytheism and animism. Leah Kalmanson offers a new approach to understanding the world's varied religious traditions: a philosophy of spiritual diversity. *Local Gods* foregrounds the numinous, subtle, and supernormal factors that pervade many aspects of everyday life but slip through the cracks of philosophical discourse on religion.

LEAH KALMANSON is an associate professor and the Bhagwan Adinath Professor of Jain Studies in the Department of Philosophy and Religion at the University of North Texas. She is the author of *Cross-Cultural Existentialism: On the Meaning of Life in Asian and Western Thought* (2020) and coauthor of *A Practical Guide to World Philosophies: Selves, Worlds, and Ways of Knowing* (2021).

$28.00 / £22.00 paper 978-0-231-21543-5
$110.00 / £85.00 cloth 978-0-231-21542-8

MARCH 216 pages / 5.5" x 8.5"

RELIGION

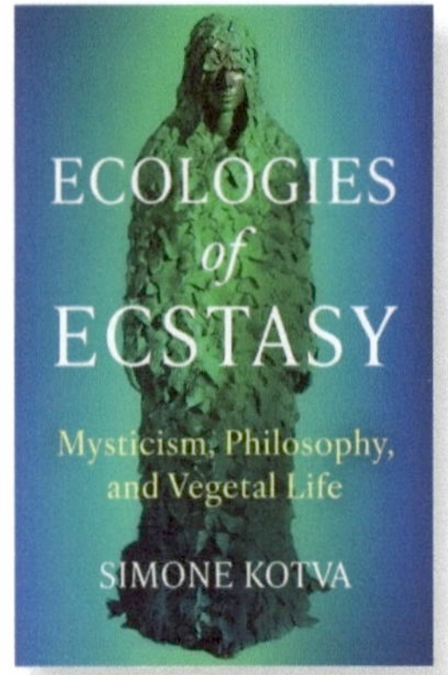

Ecologies of Ecstasy

Mysticism, Philosophy, and Vegetal Life

SIMONE KOTVA

"Kotva does not just trace a deep, startlingly earthy theological history of vegetal contemplation but grows a vibrant green hybrid of Christian mysticism and the plant life of our planet."

—Catherine Keller, author of *No Matter What: Crisis and the Spirit of Planetary Possibility*

What might religious practice learn from plants? *Ecologies of Ecstasy* recasts religious contemplation as a form of vegetal being, arguing that spiritual practice is rooted in the generation of life on earth. Simone Kotva explores the role of vegetal life in the history of Christian mysticism and the practice of contemplation, demonstrating its significance to the concept of mystical union, which rests on the loss of distinction between self and world.

SIMONE KOTVA is a senior lecturer in the Department of Literature, History of Ideas, and Religion at the University of Gothenburg. She is the author of *Effort and Grace: On the Spiritual Exercise of Philosophy* (2020).

$35.00 / £28.00 paper 978-0-231-21397-4
$140.00 / £108.00 cloth 978-0-231-21396-7

FEBRUARY 288 pages / 5.5" x 8.5" / 1 b&w illustration

RELIGION

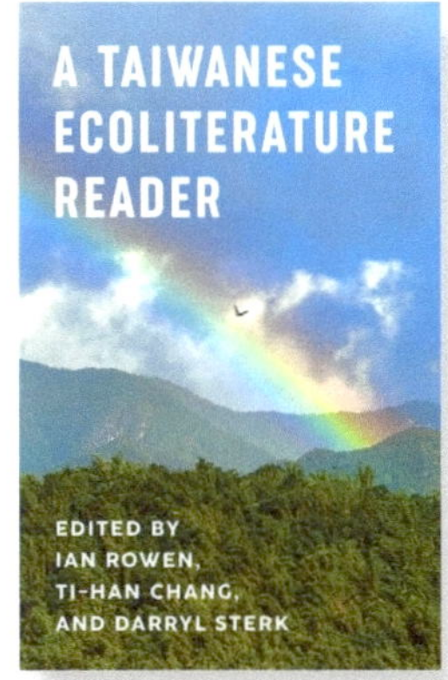

A Taiwanese Ecoliterature Reader

IAN ROWEN, TI-HAN CHANG, AND DARRYL STERK, EDITORS

"A welcoming and authoritative introduction to one of the world's richest traditions of environmental storytelling."

—Scott Slovic, Oregon Research Institute, coeditor of *Ecocriticism in Taiwan*

This anthology showcases cutting-edge works on ecological themes by essential and emerging Taiwanese authors, revealing the vitality of their engagements with environmental crises. Works included span Indigenous eco-writing, oceanic hybrid narratives, ecological sci-fi, and speculative Indigenous fiction.

IAN ROWEN is an associate professor in the Institute for Advanced Study at Kyushu University.

TI-HAN CHANG is a senior teaching fellow and the deputy director of the Centre of Taiwan Studies at SOAS, University of London.

DARRYL STERK is an associate professor of translation at Lingnan University.

$30.00 / £25.00 paper 978-0-231-22238-9
$120.00 / £100.00 cloth 978-0-231-22237-2

AVAILABLE NOW 200 pages / 5.5" x 8.5"

LITERATURE IN TRANSLATION

World English-language Rights: Columbia University Press; All Other Rights: National Museum of Taiwan Literature

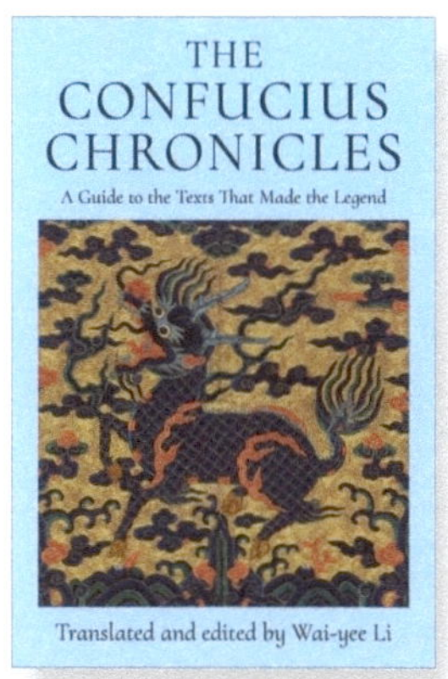

The Confucius Chronicles

A Guide to the Texts That Made the Legend

WAI-YEE LI, EDITOR AND TRANSLATOR

"Confucius is among the most admired—and most debated—figures in Chinese history. Li introduces this polyphony through annotated translations of a variety of stories, from Confucius's biography to a recent internet song. Students and scholars alike will enjoy this book immensely."

—Yuri Pines, author of *Zhou History Unearthed: The Bamboo Manuscript* Xinian *and Early Chinese Historiography*

This book explores enduring narratives about Confucius, shedding light on his role as a symbol of cultural ideals and a fulcrum of ideological debates across eras. Wai-yee Li translates and provides commentary on a wide range of key texts, examining how Confucius's legacy was interpreted in different historical moments. Suitable for a range of courses, this book offers new ways to understand Chinese cultural and intellectual history through Confucius and his transformations.

WAI-YEE LI is the 1879 Professor of Chinese Literature at Harvard University. Her recent books include *Gender and Friendship in Chinese Literature* (2024).

$35.00 / £28.00 paper 978-0-231-21483-4
$140.00 / £108.00 cloth 978-0-231-21482-7

JANUARY 368 pages / 6" x 9" / 9 b&w figures

ASIAN STUDIES

All Rights: Columbia University Press

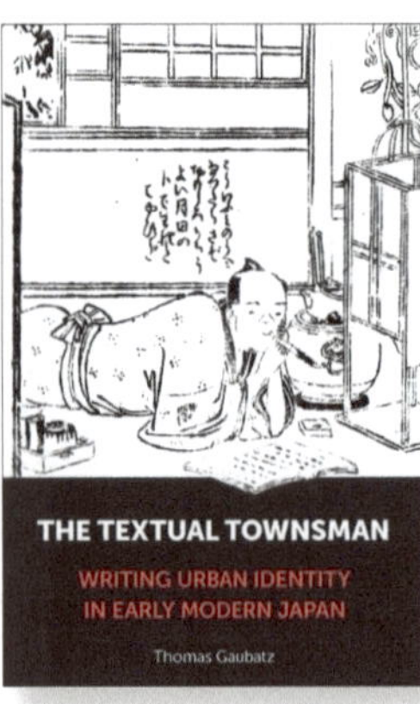

The Textual Townsman

Writing Urban Identity in Early Modern Japan

THOMAS GAUBATZ

"*The Textual Townsman* heralds a bright new age for the study of early modern Japanese literature. Gaubatz harnesses a deep knowledge of Edo's urban history to his exemplary skills as a critic and translator to bring key texts and the city they represented to rich, complex life."

—David L. Howell, author of *Geographies of Identity in Nineteenth-Century Japan*

In this innovative and interdisciplinary book, Thomas Gaubatz offers a fresh approach to understanding the literature of the Tokugawa townspeople. Ranging across history, literature, and print culture, he shows that popular fiction made sense of the urban world by modeling how individuals could refashion themselves through the performance of shared norms. Through this vision of textual self-fashioning, *The Textual Townsman* develops a radically new account of the politics of popular fiction in Tokugawa status society.

THOMAS GAUBATZ is assistant professor of Japanese literature and culture at Northwestern University.

$37.00 / £30.00 paper 978-0-231-22131-3
$145.00 / £121.00 cloth 978-0-231-22130-6
AVAILABLE NOW 344 pages / 6" x 9" / 10 b&w illustrations
ASIAN STUDIES

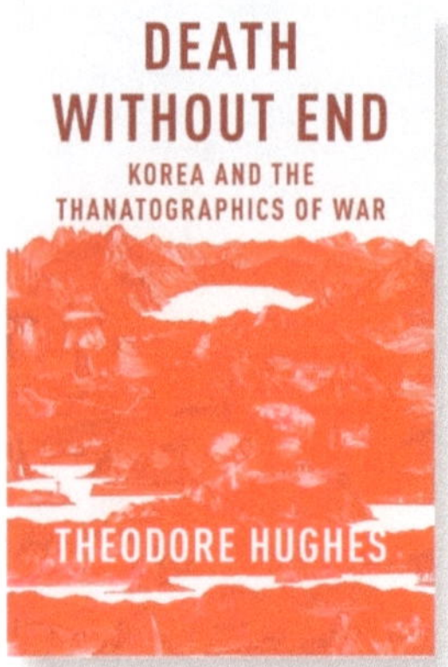

Death Without End

Korea and the Thanatographics of War

THEODORE HUGHES

"An instant classic that brilliantly unpacks the thanatographic imagination sustaining limitless war in the militarized transpacific."

—Youngju Ryu, author of *Writers of the Winter Republic: Literature and Resistance in Park Chung Hee's Korea*

Theodore Hughes crosses borders to demonstrate how stories of dying and death—what he calls the thanatographic imagination—in North Korea, the United States, and South Korea energize ideas about history, the present, and the future. He shows how literary texts, films, nonfiction, and other forms of cultural production from the late 1940s to the 1960s address the incommensurate loss of life, violence, destruction, and suffering of the war. Bridging Korean studies, American studies, and the cultural turn in international relations, this book offers new ways to understand the unending Korean War and the global implications of its logic of limitlessness.

THEODORE HUGHES is the Korea Foundation Professor of Korean Studies in the Humanities at Columbia University. He is the author of *Literature and Film in Cold War South Korea: Freedom's Frontier* (Columbia, 2012).

$35.00 / £28.00 paper 978-0-231-18607-0
$140.00 / £108.00 cloth 978-0-231-18606-3
FEBRUARY 312 pages / 6.125" x 9.25" / 59 b&w images
ASIAN STUDIES

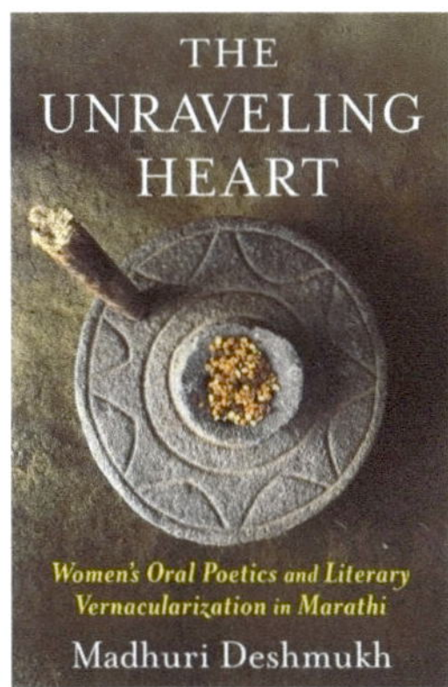

The Unraveling Heart

Women's Oral Poetics and Literary Vernacularization in Marathi

MADHURI DESHMUKH

"Deshmukh sheds a brilliant light on the lives and songs of women enslaved, marginalized, and forgotten over centuries. *The Unraveling Heart* is a major literary achievement."

—Manan Ahmed Asif, author of *The Loss of Hindustan: The Invention of India*

Women's songs of the grind mill are among the oldest oral traditions in South Asia. Madhuri Deshmukh shows that these songs played a foundational role in the vernacular turn to making literature in Marathi between the thirteenth and eighteenth centuries. She calls for understanding these artfully crafted compositions as oral poetry in a lyric mode, underscoring that women describe their songs as an "unraveling of the heart" while they compare written poetry to weaving. *The Unraveling Heart* offers new insight into the importance of labor and gender to aesthetics and develops a novel approach to the concept of the literary.

MADHURI DESHMUKH is professor of English at Oakton College.

$37.00 / £30.00 paper 978-0-231-21792-7
$150.00 / £125.00 cloth 978-0-231-21793-4

AVAILABLE NOW 360 pages / 6" x 9" / 28 b&w illustrations

LITERARY STUDIES

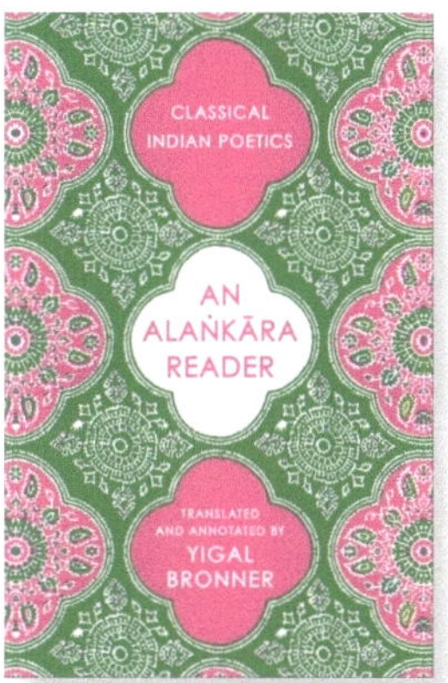

An Alaṅkāra Reader

Classical Indian Poetics

TRANSLATED AND ANNOTATED BY YIGAL BRONNER

"A pioneering work that will change the study of premodern South Asian intellectual history."

—David Shulman, author of *Tamil: A Biography*

Classical Indian poetics prized the skillful use of *alaṅkāras*, or "ornaments"—literary figures of speech. Sanskrit writers developed and elaborated an account of literary embellishment that is perhaps the world's most complex and long-standing theory of figuration. *An Alaṅkāra Reader* is a groundbreaking panoramic overview of this tradition, presenting extensive and accessible translations of key works that span its history, from the sixth century CE to the eighteenth. It is an essential resource for the study of classical Indian thought and the intellectual history of South Asia.

YIGAL BRONNER is a professor in the Department of Asian Studies at the Hebrew University of Jerusalem, where he teaches Sanskrit and South Asian intellectual history. His books include *A Lasting Vision: Dandin's* Mirror *in the World of Asian Letters* (2023).

$40.00 / £35.00 paper 978-0-231-22426-0
$160.00 / £134.00 cloth 978-0-231-21998-3

APRIL 432 pages / 6.125" x 9.25"

PHILOSOPHY / LITERARY STUDIES

HISTORICAL SOURCEBOOKS IN CLASSICAL INDIAN THOUGHT

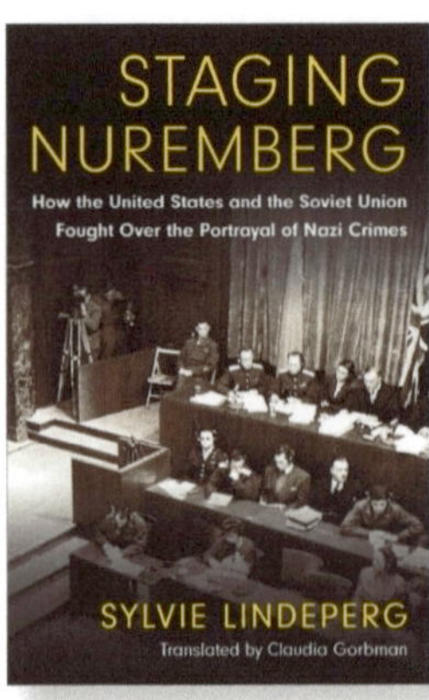

Staging Nuremberg

How the United States and the Soviet Union Fought Over the Portrayal of Nazi Crimes

SYLVIE LINDEPERG

Translated by Claudia Gorbman

"An essential work on the role of documentary in writing contemporary history."

—Ivone Margulies, author of *In Person: Reenactment in Postwar and Contemporary Cinema*

Sylvie Lindeperg offers a pioneering account of the cinematic stagecraft, storytelling, and imagery of the Nuremberg trials, revealing how film was used both as legal evidence and as a propaganda tool. She interweaves in-depth reconstruction of the filming of the trial with portraits of the colorful characters who played leading or supporting roles.

SYLVIE LINDEPERG is a historian, emeritus member of the Institut Universitaire de France, and professor at the University of Paris 1 Panthéon-Sorbonne. She is the author of many books in French, and her books in English translation include *"Night and Fog": A Film in History* (2014).

CLAUDIA GORBMAN is professor emerita of film studies at the University of Washington, Tacoma, and has translated several books by Michel Chion.

$40.00 / £30.00 paper 978-0-231-21199-4
$160.00 / £125.00 cloth 978-0-231-21198-7

JULY 408 pages / 6.125" x 9.25" / 132 b&w images

FILM AND MEDIA STUDIES

INVESTIGATING VISIBLE EVIDENCE: NEW CHALLENGES FOR DOCUMENTARY

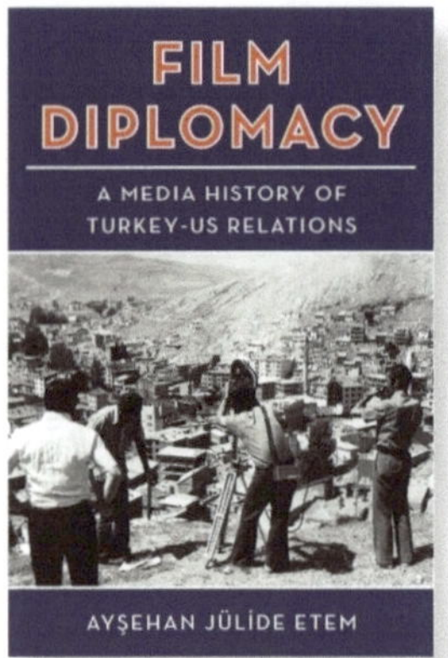

Film Diplomacy

A Media History of Turkey-US Relations

AYŞEHAN JÜLİDE ETEM

"This book is essential reading for anyone who seeks to understand Cold War cultural politics beyond the simplistic framework of 'propaganda.'"

—Perin Gürel, author of *Türkiye, Iran, and the Politics of Comparison: America's Wife, America's Concubine*

Beginning in 1930 and crystallizing during the Cold War, the United States and Turkey forged an alliance through film: American and Turkish institutions used educational films—short documentaries shown in schools, villages, theaters, and public spaces—not just to inform but to persuade. Ayşehan Jülide Etem offers a powerful new account of how film shaped international relations and national identity, demonstrating how both countries used educational films to align institutional agendas and geopolitical interests. Moving beyond conventional accounts of propaganda and soft power, this book sheds new light on media's role in global politics.

AYŞEHAN JÜLİDE ETEM is assistant professor of media studies and director of the film studies concentration at the University of Virginia.

$35.00 / £30.00 paper 978-0-231-22000-2
$140.00 / £117.00 cloth 978-0-231-21999-0

MAY 296 pages / 6" x 9" / 36 b&w illustrations

FILM AND MEDIA STUDIES

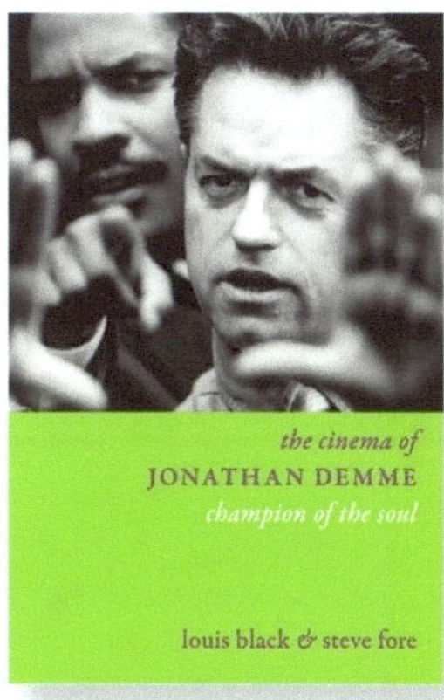

The Cinema of Jonathan Demme

Champion of the Soul

LOUIS BLACK AND STEVE FORE

Jonathan Demme was one of the most accomplished American film directors of his era, yet he remains underappreciated. This book offers an in-depth look at Demme's four decades of filmmaking, tracing the core elements that unite the disparate strands of his work. Louis Black and Steve Fore argue that Demme's films share a compassionate, emotionally generous perspective on humanity's flaws and foibles. Ranging from low-budget productions to the pinnacle of Hollywood success, this book highlights the humanist sensibility, artistic ambitions, keen social criticism, and wry humor that are hallmarks of Demme's work.

LOUIS BLACK was the longtime editor of the *Austin Chronicle* and a cofounder of South by Southwest. A film critic and historian, he has participated in the restoration and rerelease of classic Texas independent films, including Eagle Pennell's *The Whole Shootin' Match*.

STEVE FORE is retired from the School of Creative Media at the City University of Hong Kong. He previously taught at the University of North Texas, Ohio University, and the University of Texas.

$35.00 / £28.00 paper 978-0-231-22352-2
$140.00 / £108.00 cloth 978-0-231-22351-5

JUNE 368 pages / 6.125" x 9.25" / 57 film stills

FILM STUDIES

DIRECTORS' CUTS

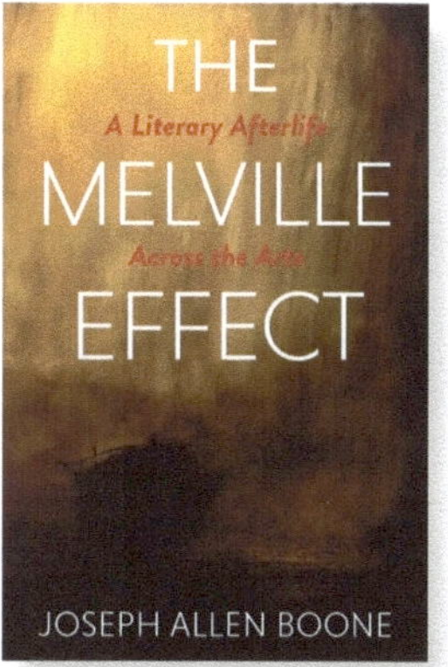

The Melville Effect

A Literary Afterlife Across the Arts

JOSEPH ALLEN BOONE

"An impressive achievement and a masterly act of literary devotion, *The Melville Effect* charts and analyzes the remarkable recent acceleration in multimedia and mixed-media responses to Melville's prose."

—Samuel Otter, author of *Melville's Anatomies*

Charting how a vast variety of writers, filmmakers, and artists channel Herman Melville, Joseph Allen Boone offers new insights into the author, his works, and his many legacies. He argues that contemporary artists are drawn to Melville's patchwork aesthetics, especially his mingling of genres and media and his prolific borrowings from popular and high culture. Boone's cases range from artists drawing on the use of whalebone in nineteenth-century fashion to critique gender roles to those obsessed, like Melville, with size and monumentality in ever-proliferating artworks.

JOSEPH ALLEN BOONE is professor emeritus of English at the University of Southern California. His recent books include *The Homoerotics of Orientalism* (Columbia, 2014), the novel *Furnace Creek* (2022), and the story collection *Conditions of Precarity* (2024).

$45.00* / £38.00 paper 978-0-231-22220-4
$180.00 / £150.00 cloth 978-0-231-22219-8

MARCH 336 pages / 6.125" x 9.25" / 96 b&w illustrations

LITERARY STUDIES

LITERARY STUDIES

American Literature's War on Crime

Novels and the Hidden History of Mass Incarceration

THEODORE MARTIN

"With breathtaking scope, *American Literature's War on Crime* argues convincingly that detective novels, vigilante narratives, and serial killer stories were instrumental to changes in policing and public policy. A remarkable book."

—Justin Gifford, author of *Revolution or Death: The Story of Eldridge Cleaver*

While the United States was building the world's largest prison system, Americans were reading crime novels. Theodore Martin offers a groundbreaking account of the ways that reading habits and crime politics intersected in the age of mass incarceration. He analyzes dozens of novels—from best-sellers to cult classics and forgotten mass-market paperbacks—by authors including James Ellroy, Ralph Ellison, Sue Grafton, Patricia Highsmith, Chester Himes, Stephen King, and Walter Mosley.

THEODORE MARTIN is associate professor of English at the University of California, Irvine. He is the author of *Contemporary Drift: Genre, Historicism, and the Problem of the Present* (Columbia, 2017).

$35.00 / £28.00 paper 978-0-231-21181-9
$140.00 / £108.00 cloth 978-0-231-21180-2

MARCH 320 pages / 6" x 9"

LITERARY STUDIES

LITERATURE NOW

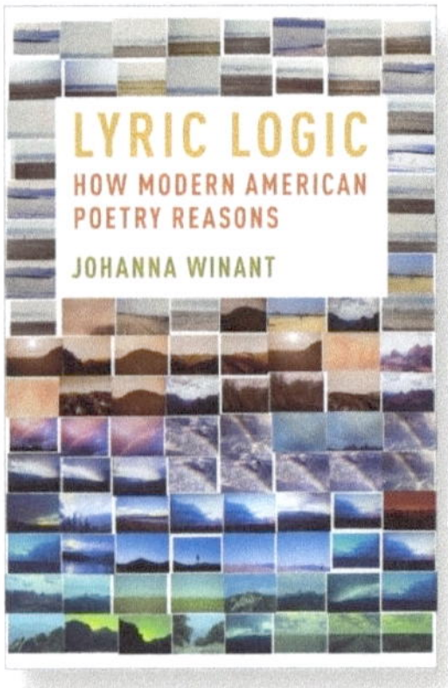

Lyric Logic

How Modern American Poetry Reasons

JOHANNA WINANT

"*Lyric Logic* is a pleasure to think with."

—Oren Izenberg, author of *Being Numerous: Poetry and the Ground of Social Life*

Between the Civil War and the Cold War, American literary modernism and philosophy both grappled with the challenge of novelty and the chance to make it new. Bringing together modern poetry's aesthetic experimentation and modern philosophy's attention to the problem of induction, *Lyric Logic* argues that poems use logical form as literary form. Johanna Winant recasts the poetics of central figures as modeling and defending inductive reasoning: Walt Whitman makes lists, Emily Dickinson constructs analogies, Gertrude Stein presents facts, Marianne Moore investigates predictions, Elizabeth Bishop draws inferences, and Gwendolyn Brooks tests the limits of deduction.

JOHANNA WINANT is associate professor of English and humanities at Reed College. She is coeditor, with Dan Sinykin, of *Close Reading for the Twenty-First Century* (2025).

$32.00 / £25.00 paper 978-0-231-21747-7
$130.00 / £100.00 cloth 978-0-231-21746-0

APRIL 344 pages / 6" x 9"

LITERARY STUDIES

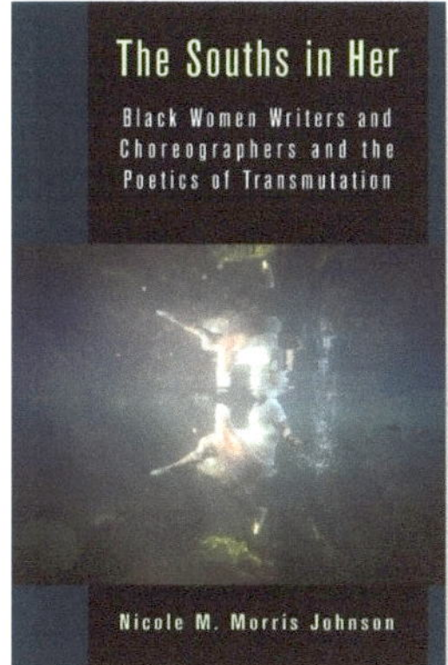

The Souths in Her

Black Women Writers and Choreographers and the Poetics of Transmutation

NICOLE M. MORRIS JOHNSON

"Beautifully written . . . An outstanding and exciting achievement in Southern studies."

—Riché Richardson, author of *Emancipation's Daughters: Reimagining Black Femininity and the National Body*

In *The Souths in Her*—a phrase borrowed from Ntozake Shange—Nicole M. Morris Johnson shows how key Black women artists transformed the enclosing narrative frames imposed on them, developing new forms of creative expression informed by the lived experiences and submerged histories of women across the Africana southern world. She analyzes the intertwined relationship between movement and writing in the works of Zora Neale Hurston, Katherine Dunham, Dianne McIntyre, Maryse Condé, and Shange, among others. For these writers and choreographers, unexpected encounters with unfamiliar traditions and creative visions of multiple Souths catalyzed formal experimentation and movements for liberation.

NICOLE M. MORRIS JOHNSON is assistant professor of English at the University at Buffalo.

$35.00 / £30.00 paper 978-0-231-21968-6
$140.00 / £117.00 cloth 978-0-231-21967-9

JANUARY 272 pages / 6" x 9" / 10 b&w illustrations

LITERARY STUDIES

BLACK LIVES IN THE DIASPORA: PAST / PRESENT / FUTURE

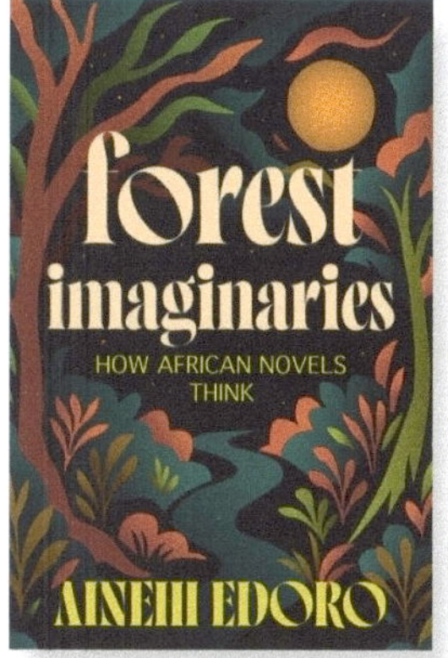

Forest Imaginaries

How African Novels Think

AINEHI EDORO

"Avoiding the parochial and the polemical, Ainehi Edoro has found a new way to write about the African novel through the paradigm of forests. This is an important contribution to the critical discourse of one of the most significant literatures of our times."

—Ben Okri, author of *The Last Gift of the Master Artists: A Novel*

Forests in fiction are often understood simply as settings, symbols, or remnants of a premodern past. Yet many African novelists have turned to the forest to experiment with worldbuilding and to imagine new futures. This groundbreaking book explores the life of the forest in African fiction, showing how writers have used it to reinvent the novel's formal, aesthetic, and political possibilities. Ainehi Edoro argues that instead of treating the forest as a backdrop, these writers imagine it as a living structure: a space where politics, history, myth, violence, technology, and magic animate fictional worlds.

AINEHI EDORO is a Mellon-Morgridge Assistant Professor of English and African cultural studies at the University of Wisconsin–Madison. She is the founding editor of *Brittle Paper*, a leading platform for African literary culture.

$35.00 / £30.00 paper 978-0-231-22075-0
$140.00 / £117.00 cloth 978-0-231-22074-3

JANUARY 304 pages / 6" x 9"

LITERARY STUDIES

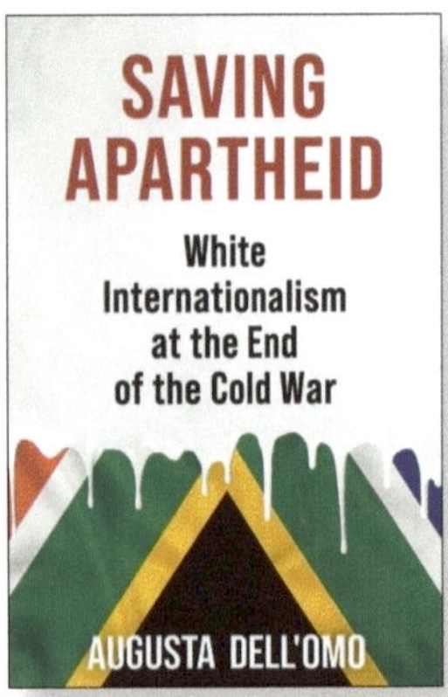

Saving Apartheid

White Internationalism at the End of the Cold War

AUGUSTA DELL'OMO

This groundbreaking book tells the story of how a transatlantic pro-apartheid movement attempted to defend white rule in South Africa—and forged enduring links between global conservatism and white power. By mapping an international network of white supremacist organizations, Augusta Dell'Omo reveals a fundamental shift in far-right organizing in response to changing geopolitical realities. *Saving Apartheid* ranges from Reagan's Oval Office to South Africa's bantustans and from white women's grassroots organizing to evangelical broadcasting, illuminating how an unlikely coalition reimagined white supremacy. Uncovering the surprising influence of apartheid's defenders, this book offers a prehistory of the present.

AUGUSTA DELL'OMO is a historian of global conservatism and the far right. She received her PhD from the University of Texas at Austin and is currently a senior fellow at the Center for Presidential History at Southern Methodist University.

$38.00 / £32.00 paper 978-0-231-21589-3
$150.00 / £125.00 cloth 978-0-231-21588-6

MARCH 384 pages / 6" x 9" / 1 b&w map

HISTORY

GLOBAL AMERICA

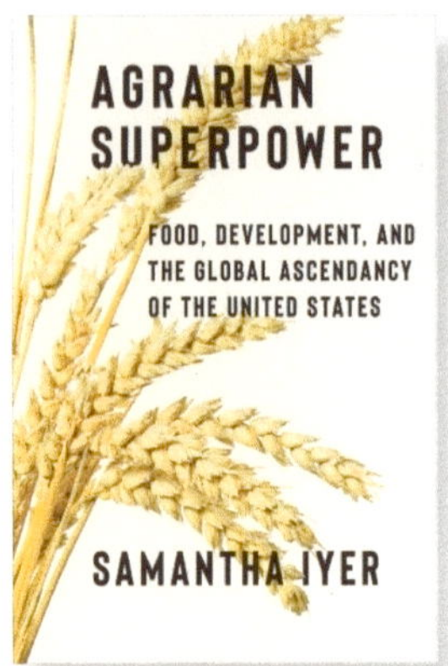

Agrarian Superpower

Food, Development, and the Global Ascendancy of the United States

SAMANTHA IYER

"A landmark work of global political economy. Iyer's commanding ambitious sweep is matched by an empirically meticulous mapping of the geographies of power that remade agrarian capitalism across the United States, Egypt, and India. A tour de force!"

—Manu Goswami, coeditor of *Political Imaginaries in Twentieth-Century India*

The United States superpower status is often associated with its industrial, financial, and military might. Yet its global power after the Second World War hinged in part on something often seen as backward: agriculture. During the 1950s, an era of decolonization and rising Cold War competition, the United States became the dominant exporter of food staples to industrializing nations in the Third World through its massive food aid program. Through the lens of food and agriculture, this book offers new ways to understand the roots of the postwar global order and the US position in it.

SAMANTHA IYER is associate professor of history at Fordham University.

$36.00 / £28.00 paper 978-0-231-21503-9
$145.00 / £112.00 cloth 978-0-231-21502-2

MARCH 368 pages / 6" x 9" / 17 b&w illustrations

HISTORY

GLOBAL AMERICA

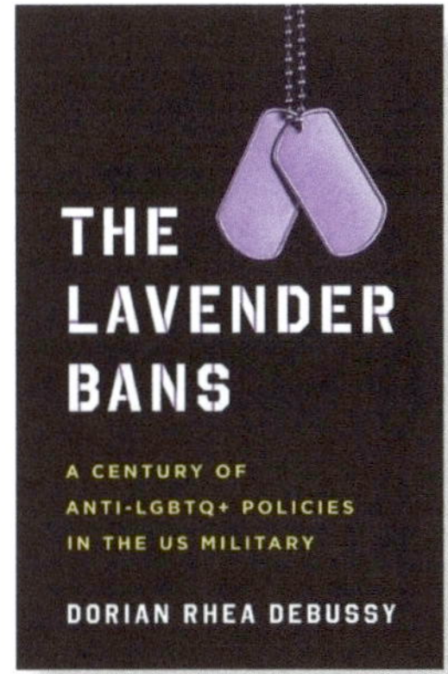

The Lavender Bans

A Century of Anti-LGBTQ+ Policies in the US Military

DORIAN RHEA DEBUSSY

"This book confronts the ever-shifting rationales for banning LGBTQ+ military service—often contradicted by the government's own data—with rigor and clarity."

—Bree Fram, Col. (Ret.), US Space Force

This book is a comprehensive account of the evolution of anti-LGBTQ+ policies from World War I to the present. Dorian Rhea Debussy examines six distinct periods of exclusion over the course of a century, tracing continuities and changes alongside the growth of the national security state. Meticulously researched and rich in detail, *The Lavender Bans* sheds light on a long and troubling history—with deep contemporary relevance. It is an engaging, important, and timely book for a range of readers, including scholars, students, policy makers, military personnel, and people affected by anti-LGBTQ+ discrimination.

DORIAN RHEA DEBUSSY is the director of external affairs at Equitas Health. A nationally recognized expert in LGBTQ+ politics, she specializes in healthcare and defense policy. Debussy is a lecturer in women's, gender, and sexuality studies at the Ohio State University.

$32.00 / £28.00 paper 978-0-231-20575-7
$130.00 / £108.00 cloth 978-0-231-20574-0

MARCH 240 pages / 6" x 9"

HISTORY / LGBTQ+ STUDIES

Jimmy Carter and China

Multilateral Competition in the Global Cold War

SHENG PENG

This book is an international history of the Carter administration's intricate relations with the two competing Chinese regimes, emphasizing the geopolitical significance and lasting implications of this crucial moment. Drawing extensively from previously untapped archives in several countries and languages, Sheng Peng uncovers the internal governmental debates across world capitals that affected Carter's China policy. He demonstrates that technological competition was as crucial as strategic and ideological competition to the course of the Cold War, and together they profoundly shaped US-China relations and the world today.

SHENG PENG is a postdoctoral fellow at the Research Center for the History of Transformations at the University of Vienna and an associate fellow at Harvard Kennedy School's Belfer Center for Science and International Affairs.

$35.00 / £30.00 paper 978-0-231-21195-6
$140.00 / £117.00 cloth 978-0-231-21194-9

MARCH 328 pages / 6" x 9" / 20 b&w illustrations

HISTORY

A NANCY BERNKOPF TUCKER AND WARREN I. COHEN BOOK ON AMERICAN-EAST ASIAN RELATIONS

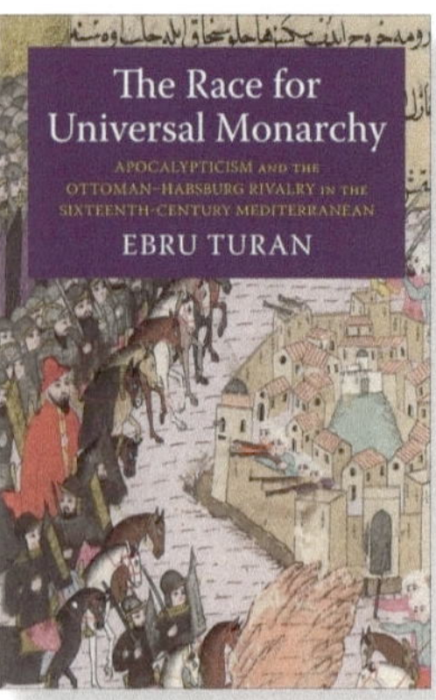

The Race for Universal Monarchy

Apocalypticism and the Ottoman–Habsburg Rivalry in the Sixteenth-Century Mediterranean

EBRU TURAN

"This impressive book recasts the sixteenth-century confrontation between Suleyman the Magnificent and Charles V against the background of a much wider political theater and a much longer history of apocalyptic and millenarian thought. Both specialists and general readers will learn a great deal from this book's balanced yet intricate narrative."

—Giancarlo Casale, professor of early modern history of the Mediterranean, European University Institute

The early sixteenth century saw the rise of two Mediterranean empires—the Christian Habsburgs and the Muslim Ottomans—with strikingly similar ambitions to usher in an age of peace, unity, and justice. Drawing on a wide range of Ottoman and European sources, Ebru Turan explores the emergence of these empires and the early phase of their rivalry within the broader Mediterranean world.

EBRU TURAN is assistant professor of history at Fordham University.

$40.00 / £35.00 paper 978-0-231-21926-6
$160.00 / £134.00 cloth 978-0-231-21925-9

APRIL 400 pages / 6" x 9" / 36 b&w illustrations

HISTORY

COLUMBIA STUDIES IN INTERNATIONAL AND GLOBAL HISTORY

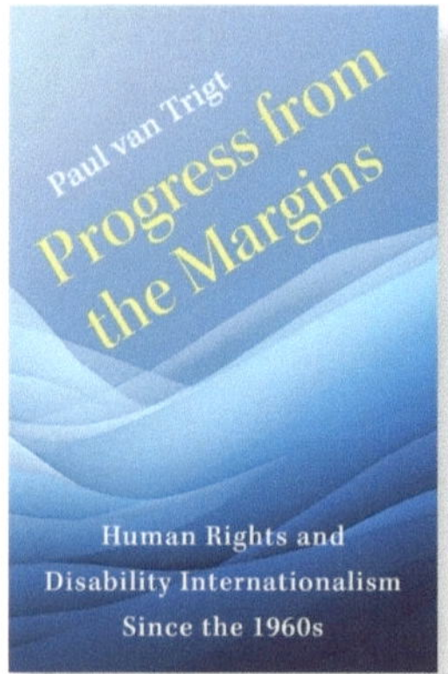

Progress from the Margins

Human Rights and Disability Internationalism Since the 1960s

PAUL VAN TRIGT

"This excellent study goes far beyond merely placing the struggle for disability rights in the broader story of human rights. The two transformed each other, *Progress from the Margins* shows."

—Samuel Moyn, author of *The Last Utopia: Human Rights in History*

This book is an international history of the struggle for recognition of disability rights at the global level. Paul van Trigt chronicles how people with disabilities and their allies developed their own understanding of human rights, from the emergence of disability activism in the late 1960s through the negotiation of the 2006 United Nations Convention on the Rights of Persons with Disabilities. A groundbreaking account of disability internationalism, *Progress from the Margins* also reflects on the prospects for a world that embraces disability.

PAUL VAN TRIGT is assistant professor of social history at Leiden University. He is a coeditor of *Marginalized Groups, Inequalities and the Post-War Welfare State: Whose Welfare?* (2020).

$32.00 / £28.00 paper 978-0-231-21993-8
$130.00 / £109.00 cloth 978-0-231-21992-1

AVAILABLE NOW 224 pages / 6" x 9" / 3 b&w illustrations

HISTORY

COLUMBIA STUDIES IN INTERNATIONAL AND GLOBAL HISTORY

Melancholy Borders

Mobility, Migration, and Exclusion in Global History

ANDREW B. LIU, OWEN MILLER, AND MEHA PRIYADARSHINI, EDITORS

"*Melancholy Borders* points to the many corners of the world where a modern tension between mobility and restriction illustrates contestations over power, freedom, and human autonomy not often captured in national treatments of immigration."

—Donna R. Gabaccia, general editor of *The Cambridge History of Global Migrations*

Showcasing the latest research in the burgeoning field of global migration history, this book explores the historical clash between transnational networks of migrant mobility with state attempts to control them. *Melancholy Borders* illuminates the crucial role played by migration and migration regulation in the creation of the modern world.

ANDREW B. LIU is associate professor of history at Villanova University.

OWEN MILLER is assistant professor of history at Bilkent University.

MEHA PRIYADARSHINI is senior lecturer in history at the University of Edinburgh.

$35.00 / £30.00 paper 978-0-231-20719-5
$140.00 / £115.00 cloth 978-0-231-20718-8

MAY 376 pages / 6" x 9" / 2 b&w illustrations

HISTORY

COLUMBIA STUDIES IN INTERNATIONAL AND GLOBAL HISTORY

Linguistic Resistance in Pakistan

Punjabi Language Movements After Independence

JULIEN COLUMEAU

"Columeau shows us the complexity of the various movements that emerged in support of Punjabi in Pakistan in the two decades after Partition/Independence, providing a rich account of not only key figures in these movements but also the writings, ideologies, and activities associated with them."

—Anne Murphy, University of British Columbia

Soon after independence, the Pakistani government adopted a language policy that promoted the use of Urdu. In Punjab, intellectuals launched three separate movements for the defense and promotion of Punjabi, divided along the lines of their political and literary affiliations: Marxists, conservatives, and modernists. *Linguistic Resistance in Pakistan* examines these three movements, taking an interdisciplinary perspective that combines sociological, historical, political, and literary approaches.

JULIEN COLUMEAU holds a PhD in history from the École des hautes études en sciences sociales and is currently affiliated with the Centre d'études sud-asiatiques et himalayennes. He has published five books of fiction in Urdu, and his short story "Derrida in Lahore" received the Susannah Hunnewell Prize from the *Paris Review*.

$35.00 / £30.00 paper 978-0-231-21982-2
$140.00 / £117.00 cloth 978-0-231-21981-5

MARCH 288 pages / 6" x 9"

HISTORY

POLITICS

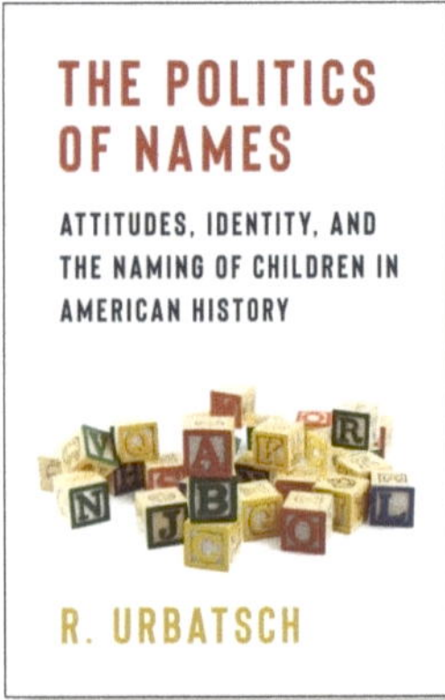

The Politics of Names

Attitudes, Identity, and the Naming of Children in American History

R. URBATSCH

"A masterpiece of innovative, nontraditional social science research. Creative, insightful, and entertaining throughout, this engaging book convincingly establishes why names are an important measure for understanding political development across time."

—Adam Chamberlain, Coastal Carolina University

R. Urbatsch explores the politics of naming across American history, revealing the surprising ways parents' choices shed light on public opinion past and present. He argues that naming is a weathervane for political attitudes: Names touch on every sort of identity, from race and gender to nationalism and religion. By analyzing when politics-tinged names gained or lost popularity, this book offers an unconventional and illuminating new perspective on identity, public sentiment, and political behavior in the United States.

R. URBATSCH is professor of political science at Iowa State University. He is the author of *Families' Values: How Parents, Siblings, and Children Affect Political Attitudes* (2014).

$32.00 / £28.00 paper 978-0-231-22169-6
$130.00 / £109.00 cloth 978-0-231-22168-9

JANUARY 272 pages / 6" x 9" / 53 b&w illustrations

POLITICS

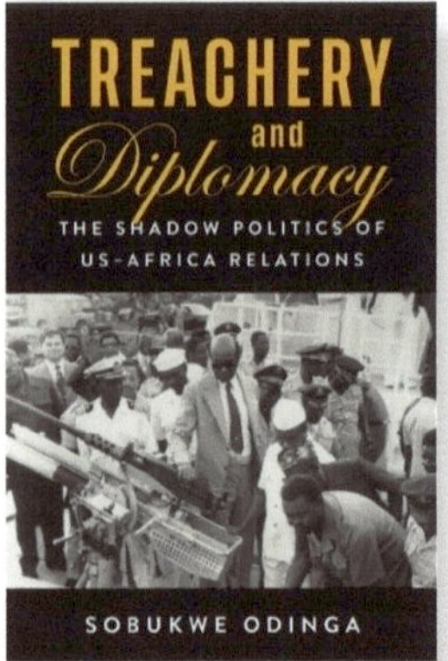

Treachery and Diplomacy

The Shadow Politics of US-Africa Relations

SOBUKWE ODINGA

The African allies of the United States are often depicted as mere pawns or clients seeking aid. Yet African leaders have deftly capitalized on security partnerships with the United States in ways that have been widely overlooked. *Treachery and Diplomacy* shines a light on US-Africa security partnerships, revealing their simmering internal tensions, hidden racial politics, and consequences for peace and democracy. Sobukwe Odinga explores the contentious relations between the United States and key African allies—Liberia, Ethiopia, Zaire (now the Democratic Republic of the Congo), and Uganda—from the Cold War to the War on Terror. He brings to life the diplomatic gambits of leaders such as William Tubman, Mobutu Sese Seko, and Yoweri Museveni, documenting how they prodded Washington to back them in regional conflicts, increase aid, and temper criticisms of their domestic policies.

SOBUKWE ODINGA is an assistant professor in the Department of African American Studies at the University of California, Los Angeles.

$35.00 / £30.00 paper 978-0-231-20269-5
$140.00 / £115.00 cloth 978-0-231-20268-8

MARCH 312 pages / 6" x 9"

POLITICS

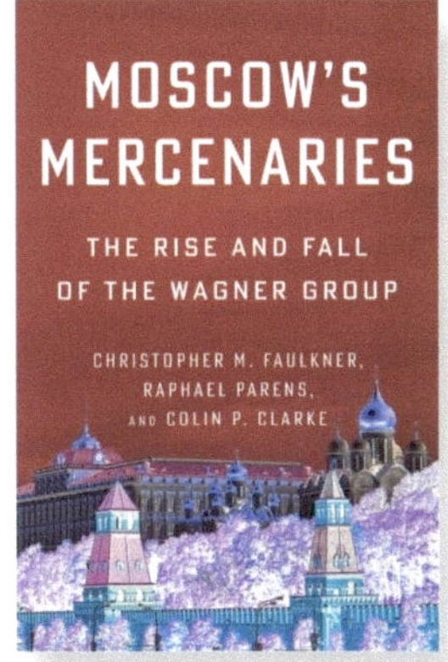

Moscow's Mercenaries

The Rise and Fall of the Wagner Group

CHRISTOPHER M. FAULKNER, RAPHAEL PARENS, AND COLIN P. CLARKE

"A chilling and imperative account of how irregular warfare serves as a primary and expanding instrument of authoritarian power."

—Jason Warner, US Army Foreign Military Studies Office

The Wagner Group emerged from Russia's criminal underworld in 2014 and soon became one of the world's most infamous private military companies. This book traces the Wagner Group's violent ascent and descent, exposing how a shadow army built an empire until it turned on its masters.

CHRISTOPHER M. FAULKNER is an assistant professor of national security affairs at the US Naval War College and a nonresident senior fellow in the Foreign Policy Research Institute's Eurasia Program.

RAPHAEL PARENS is a fellow in the Foreign Policy Research Institute's Eurasia and Africa Programs and a senior fellow at the Delphi Global Research Center.

COLIN P. CLARKE is the executive director of the Soufan Center and a nonresident senior fellow at the Foreign Policy Research Institute.

$35.00 / £30.00 paper 978-0-231-21690-6
$140.00 / £117.00 cloth 978-0-231-21691-3

JULY 368 pages / 6" x 9" / 4 b&w illustrations

POLITICS / SECURITY STUDIES

COLUMBIA STUDIES IN TERRORISM AND IRREGULAR WARFARE

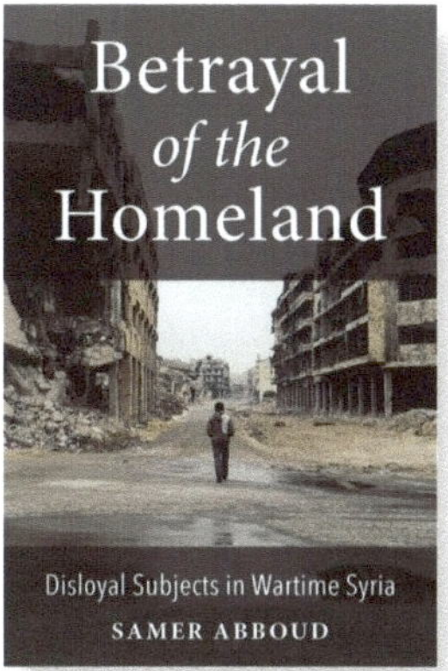

Betrayal of the Homeland

Disloyal Subjects in Wartime Syria

SAMER ABBOUD

"Abboud offers a groundbreaking analysis of how the Assad regime transformed warfare into statecraft in Syria. This book is essential reading for anyone interested in how modern authoritarian regimes sustain illiberal peace through violence."

—Marwa Daoudy, Georgetown University

Samer Abboud argues that the Syrian regime sought to entrench its rule during wartime through bifurcating society into "loyal" and "disloyal" subjects—and punishing those it deemed treacherous. It established new laws, courts, and legal categories that targeted "betrayal," which could include anything from military desertion to absenteeism to critical social media posts. *Betrayal of the Homeland* offers a panoramic view of the politics of punishment during the final decade of the Assad regime, with broader implications for understanding how authoritarian states manage conflicts.

SAMER ABBOUD is associate professor of global interdisciplinary studies and director of the Center for Arab and Islamic Studies at Villanova University. He is the author of *Syria* (second edition, 2018).

$35.00 / £30.00 paper 978-0-231-21533-6
$140.00 / £117.00 cloth 978-0-231-21532-9

MARCH 256 pages / 6" x 9"

POLITICS

COLUMBIA STUDIES IN MIDDLE EAST POLITICS

Adversary and Ally

How China Shapes the Frontier Politics of India and Pakistan

HARRISON AKINS

Connecting international politics with domestic security, Harrison Akins shows how India and Pakistan's engagement with China has shaped the two governments' policies toward their strategic frontiers over the past seventy years. He demonstrates that China's presence spurred the Indian and Pakistani governments to assert their sovereignty over key border regions, exacerbating conditions that led to the outbreak of antistate violence. Featuring comprehensive research and keen analysis, *Adversary and Ally* offers new insights into the pressures confronting South Asian governments and the limits of China's reach.

HARRISON AKINS is a political scientist and writer who holds a PhD from the University of Tennessee, Knoxville. For more than a decade, he has been researching, writing, and advising on South Asian politics and US foreign policy in both academia and government. His books include *The Terrorism Trap: How the War on Terror Escalates Violence in America's Partner States* (Columbia, 2023).

$35.00 / £30.00 paper 978-0-231-22182-5
$140.00 / £117.00 cloth 978-0-231-22181-8
FEBRUARY 312 pages / 6" x 9" / 2 b&w illustrations
POLITICS

Make China Great Again

Online Alt-History Fiction and Popular Authoritarianism

RONGBIN HAN

"A pathbreaking study of digital pop culture as everyday ideology and politics."

—Guobin Yang, author of *The Wuhan Lockdown*

On the Chinese internet, alternate history is booming. Millions of writers and readers fantasize about going back in time and changing their country's fate. Rongbin Han examines the production and consumption of online alt-history fiction in China, offering new insight into how authoritarian rule gains popular consent. Combining in-depth digital ethnography with analysis of dozens of alt-history novels, he explores how state intervention, market forces, and consumer preferences interact.

RONGBIN HAN is professor of international affairs at the University of Georgia. He is the author of *Contesting Cyberspace in China: Online Expression and Authoritarian Resilience* (Columbia, 2018), coauthor of *Directed Digital Dissidence in Autocracies: How China Wins Online* (2023), and coeditor of *The Xi Jinping Effect* (2024).

$35.00 / £30.00 paper 978-0-231-22055-2
$140.00 / £117.00 cloth 978-0-231-22054-5
MARCH 240 pages / 6" x 9" / 5 b&w illustrations
POLITICS

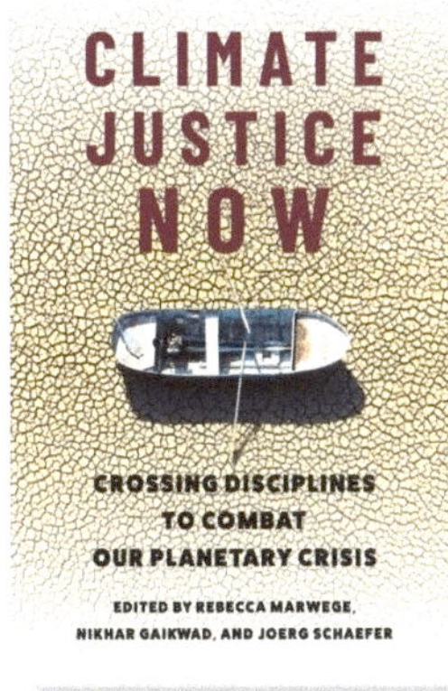

Climate Justice Now

Crossing Disciplines to Combat Our Planetary Crisis

REBECCA MARWEGE, NIKHAR GAIKWAD, AND JOERG SCHAEFER, EDITORS

"This groundbreaking book bridges knowledge silos to confront climate injustice both within and beyond academia."

—Jennifer Hadden, author of *Networks in Contention: The Divisive Politics of Climate Change*

This book offers a comprehensive exploration of debates on climate justice across the natural sciences, social sciences, and humanities, illuminating how scholarship on climate change can become a call to action.

REBECCA MARWEGE is an assistant professor of environmental politics at the American University of Paris.

NIKHAR GAIKWAD is an assistant professor of political science and a member of the Committee on Global Thought at Columbia University.

JOERG SCHAEFER is a Lamont Research Professor in the Lamont-Doherty Earth Observatory and an adjunct professor of earth and environmental sciences at Columbia University.

GAIKWAD and **SCHAEFER** are senior founding codirectors and **MARWEGE** is former junior director of the Columbia Climate School Earth Network on Decarbonization, Climate Resilience, and Climate Justice.

$38.00 / £32.00 paper 978-0-231-22024-8
$150.00 / £125.00 cloth 978-0-231-22023-1

MARCH 392 pages / 6" x 9" / 10 b&w illustrations

POLITICS / CLIMATE CHANGE

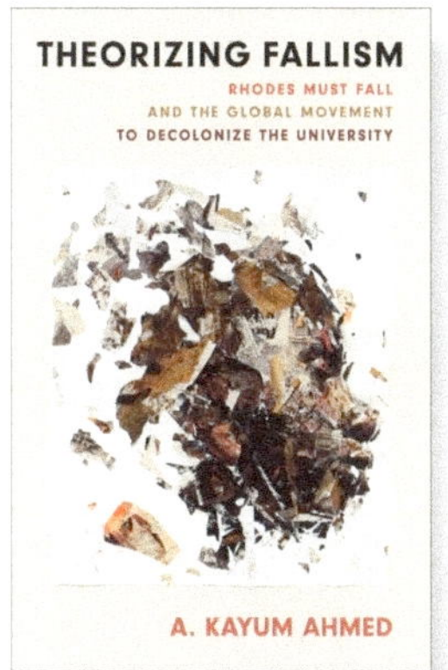

Theorizing Fallism

Rhodes Must Fall and the Global Movement to Decolonize the University

A. KAYUM AHMED

"Rich in primary source material, including the voices of student and worker activists, *Theorizing Fallism* serves as an invaluable archival resource on the evolution of the Rhodes Must Fall movements at University of Cape Town and Oxford."

—Anye-Nkwenti Nyamnjoh, University of Cape Town

In 2015, students at the University of Cape Town ignited a movement that would reverberate across the globe by demanding the removal of a statue of the British imperialist Cecil Rhodes. A. Kayum Ahmed tells the powerful story of Rhodes Must Fall, tracing the emergence of a new decolonial framework, Fallism, and its trajectory from Africa to empire. Both a history of a movement and a theoretical intervention, *Theorizing Fallism* illuminates the enduring influence of students to challenge entrenched structures of knowledge and power.

A. KAYUM AHMED is a South African activist-scholar who has taught at Columbia University and held visiting scholar roles at Birzeit University and Harvard University. He previously served as CEO of the South African Human Rights Commission.

$35.00 / £28.00 paper 978-0-231-21273-1
$140.00 / £108.00 cloth 978-0-231-21272-4

MAY 296 pages / 5.5" x 8.5"

POLITICS

BLACK LIVES IN THE DIASPORA: PAST / PRESENT / FUTURE

PHILOSOPHY

Word and Plan

JOHN MACFARLANE

"Many observers outside of philosophy are puzzled by the fact that problems about vagueness have been such a preoccupation in the philosophy of language, but *Word and Plan* explains precisely why these issues are so important. MacFarlane's arguments, both constructive and critical, are incisive and convincing."

—Robert Stalnaker, author of *Propositions: Ontology and Logic*

We commonly believe that communication is successful when a hearer grasps what a speaker means. But Abe can assert "Sam is tall" without having any definite intention about how tall one must be to count as "tall," and Bertha can understand his assertion without grasping such an intention. What exactly has been communicated in such a case? John MacFarlane argues that standard models of meaning and communication cannot answer this question. To answer it, he proposes, we need to see vague talk as not purely factual but in part expressive of linguistic plans. In this book, he gives a novel expressivist account of vagueness and explores its implications for semantics, pragmatics, thought, and disagreement.

JOHN MACFARLANE is a professor in the Department of Philosophy and the Group in Logic and the Methodology of Science at the University of California, Berkeley. He is the author of *Assessment Sensitivity: Relative Truth and Its Applications* (2014) and *Philosophical Logic: A Contemporary Introduction* (2021).

$32.00 / £28.00 paper 978-0-231-21281-6
$130.00 / £108.00 cloth 978-0-231-21280-9

MAY 224 pages / 5.5" x 8.5" / 13 b&w illustrations

PHILOSOPHY

COLUMBIA THEMES IN PHILOSOPHY

Ambivalent Recognition

The Harmful Social Consequences of an Ethical Good

KRISTINA LEPOLD

Translated by Ciaran Cronin

Foreword by Martin Saar

"A masterful study."

—Axel Honneth, coauthor of *Redistribution or Recognition? A Political-Philosophical Exchange*

In this ambitious and compelling book, Kristina Lepold challenges the common assumption that recognition is positive. Showing how recognition can implicate us in oppressive arrangements, Lepold engages with different approaches—including Axel Honneth's influential theory, as well as arguments made by Louis Althusser, Pierre Bourdieu, and Judith Butler.

KRISTINA LEPOLD is a junior professor of social philosophy and critical theory at Humboldt University Berlin and an associated member of the Center for Social Critique.

CIARAN CRONIN has translated numerous works of political philosophy and social theory by prominent authors including Jürgen Habermas and Rainer Forst.

MARTIN SAAR is professor of social philosophy at Goethe-Universität Frankfurt am Main.

$30.00 / £25.00 paper 978-0-231-21730-9
$120.00 / £100.00 cloth 978-0-231-21729-3

APRIL 248 pages / 5.5" x 8.5" / 3 b&w illustrations

PHILOSOPHY

NEW DIRECTIONS IN CRITICAL THEORY

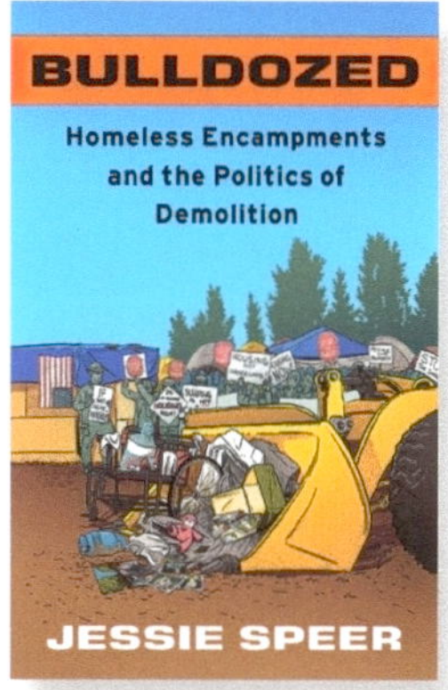

Bulldozed

Homeless Encampments and the Politics of Demolition

JESSIE SPEER

"Speer's book offers an important intervention into the possibilities of dignity and autonomy in the lives of unhoused people."

—Vincent Lyon-Callo, author of *Inequality, Poverty, and Neoliberal Governance: Activist Ethnography in the Homeless Sheltering Industry*

Jessie Speer interweaves an ethnographic account of the lives of unhoused people in Fresno, California, with an investigation of why cities across the United States have turned to what she calls the "bulldozer approach" to homelessness. She tells the powerful stories of people on the margins, painting a complex and detailed portrait of everyday life in the camps. Combining national data with more than a decade of on-the-ground research, *Bulldozed* exposes the violence of US housing politics and offers a vision of a more equal city.

JESSIE SPEER is an assistant professor in the Department of Geography and Environment at the London School of Economics and Social Science. She previously practiced law in California, working at legal aid clinics assisting people experiencing domestic violence and eviction.

$35.00 / £28.00 paper 978-0-231-21077-5
$140.00 / £108.00 cloth 978-0-231-21076-8

JUNE 320 pages / 5.5" x 8.5" / 7 b&w illustrations

SOCIOLOGY

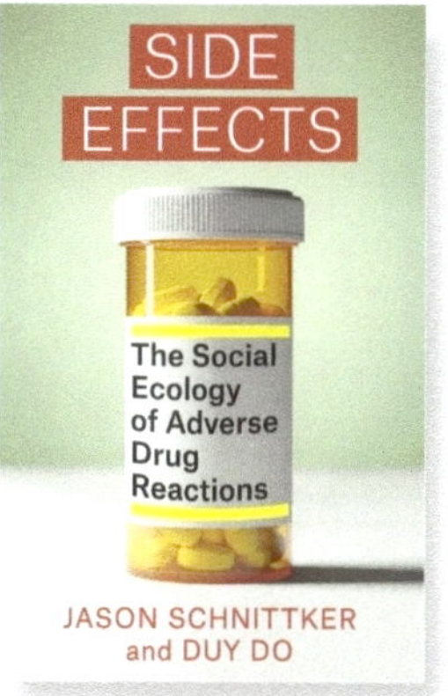

Side Effects

The Social Ecology of Adverse Drug Reactions

JASON SCHNITTKER AND DUY DO

"A deeply researched sociological appreciation of contemporary society's attempt to perceive and manage side effects."

—Stefan Timmermans, coauthor of *The Unclaimed: Abandonment and Hope in the City of Angels*

Side effects are common, but their origins and consequences remain unclear. This book uncovers the social origins of side effects and their consequences for patients, physicians, and the health care system. Jason Schnittker and Duy Do argue that side effects emerge from the interaction of cultural, institutional, and psychological factors.

JASON SCHNITTKER is a professor of sociology at the University of Pennsylvania. His previous Columbia University Press books are *The Diagnostic System: Why the Classification of Psychiatric Disorders Is Necessary, Difficult, and Never Settled* (2017) and *Unnerved: Anxiety, Social Change, and the Transformation of Modern Mental Health* (2021).

DUY DO is a senior research advisor at Evernorth Research Institute. He holds a PhD in demography from the University of Pennsylvania.

$32.00 / £28.00 paper 978-0-231-21780-4
$130.00 / £109.00 cloth 978-0-231-21779-8

MAY 360 pages / 5.5" x 8.5" / 3 b&w illustrations, 18 tables

SOCIOLOGY

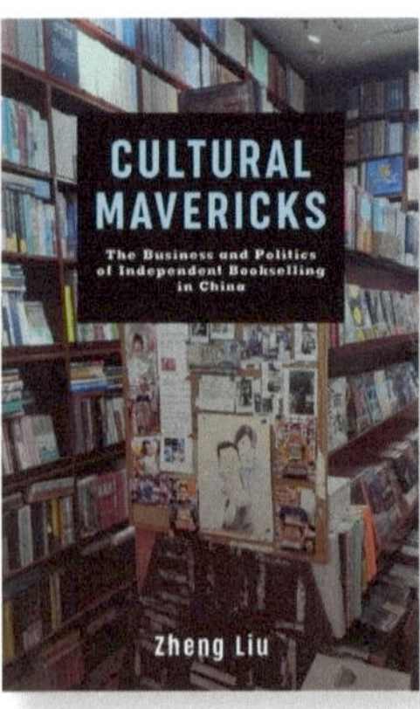

Cultural Mavericks

The Business and Politics of Independent Bookselling in China

ZHENG LIU

"A cutting-edge work of cultural sociology and a major contribution to understanding the social organization and development of one of the largest book markets in the world."

—John B. Thompson, author of *Book Wars: The Digital Revolution in Publishing*

In recent decades, self-proclaimed "independent bookstores" have arisen across China. In the West, such retailers represent an alternative to corporations and chains. In China, by contrast, they differentiate themselves from not only the state-owned Xinhua Bookstore but also other privately owned shops through an emphasis on intellectual independence and the free exchange of ideas. *Cultural Mavericks* takes readers inside the world of independent bookselling in China, showing how a wide range of figures navigate the challenges of book retailing in the digital age amid rapidly shifting social, political, and economic dynamics.

ZHENG LIU is a lecturer in innovation management at the University of Bristol Business School.

$30.00 / £25.00 paper 978-0-231-20013-4
$120.00 / £100.00 cloth 978-0-231-20012-7

JANUARY 264 pages / 5.5" x 8.5" / 23 b&w illustrations

SOCIOLOGY

Performing Public Confessions

Avowal and Disavowal of State Violence in Turkey

YEŞIM YAPRAK YILDIZ

"Timely and beautifully written, this book is a must-read for anyone interested in the Turkish state and society and those concerned about the systematic undermining of public accountability everywhere."

—Fatma Müge Göçek, University of Michigan

It is widely thought that confessions from perpetrators of state violence promote accountability, reconciliation, and justice. Yeşim Yaprak Yıldız offers a challenge to this view through a critical examination of perpetrators' narratives, analyzing them as performances that shape public perceptions of state violence and responsibility. With a focus on Turkey, this book develops new insights into the performative aspects of confessions and what they reveal about the dominant social, moral, and political order.

YEŞIM YAPRAK YILDIZ is a lecturer in sociology and program convener for the MA in human rights, culture, and social justice at Goldsmiths, University of London. She previously worked for many years with local and international human rights NGOs, and she is coeditor in chief of the *Journal of Perpetrator Research*.

$35.00 / £28.00 paper 978-0-231-22231-0
$140.00 / £108.00 cloth 978-0-231-22230-3

APRIL 288 pages / 6" x 9"

SOCIOLOGY

Cities in Action

Organizations, Institutions, and Urban Climate Strategies

CHRISTOF BRANDTNER

"This path-breaking book shows what scholars can learn if we conceive of the city as an actor, not just a stage. One of the most exciting works of urban studies I've read in years."

—Eric Klinenberg, Helen Gould Shepard Professor in the Social Sciences, New York University

As national governments and global institutions fail to address climate change, an increasing number of cities have committed to major sustainability and climate strategies. Why do some cities take bold action while others remain on the sidelines? Drawing on comparative research spanning thousands of cities around the world, Christof Brandtner uncovers the structural conditions that enable and inhibit meaningful climate action, revealing why it varies so widely. This book offers a new perspective for scholars, policy makers, and practitioners seeking not just to explain but also to empower city action.

CHRISTOF BRANDTNER is associate professor of social innovation at EM Lyon Business School, a CIFAR Fellow, and cofounder of the Civic Life of Cities Lab.

$35.00 / £30.00 paper 978-0-231-20239-8
$140.00 / £115.00 cloth 978-0-231-20238-1

FEBRUARY 336 pages / 6" x 9" / 28 b&w illustrations

SOCIOLOGY / URBAN STUDIES

SOCIETY AND THE ENVIRONMENT

Reform as Process

Implementing Change in Public Bureaucracies

MARTIN J. WILLIAMS

"In this smart and approachable book, an emerging star explains why administrative reforms succeed and fail. This book has changed the way I think about durably improving public sector performance."

—David Lewis, author of *The Politics of Presidential Appointments: Political Control and Bureaucratic Performance*

This book takes a fresh perspective on building an effective civil service by documenting and analyzing the implementation of more than one hundred reforms initiated by six African countries over the last thirty years. Martin J. Williams develops a new theory of how systemic reforms can lead to meaningful change—not by trying to force it through top-down interventions but by catalyzing an ongoing and decentralized process of continuous improvement.

MARTIN J. WILLIAMS is associate professor of organizational studies and (by courtesy) political science at the University of Michigan, as well as associate faculty at the Blavatnik School of Government, University of Oxford.

$40.00 / £35.00 paper 978-0-231-21577-0
$160.00 / £134.00 cloth 978-0-231-21576-3

FEBRUARY 400 pages / 6.125" x 9.25" / 17 b&w illustrations

POLITICS

Does Trust Matter?

Why Journalists Need to Rethink the Relationship with Their Audience

EFRAT NECHUSHTAI

"Lucid, thoughtful, and pathbreaking."

—Michael Schudson, author of *Journalism: Why It Matters*

Drawing on in-depth interviews with nearly one hundred journalists, Efrat Nechushtai shows how the desire to increase trust in the news can be weaponized to increase favorable coverage of illiberal movements. She documents how the quest for public approval has led journalists to legitimize antiscience claims in the United States, racialize crime reporting in Germany, and produce "patriotic" stories in Hungary and Israel, among other cases. Valuable for scholars and practitioners alike, this book presents practical strategies that reporters, editors, and publishers can use to navigate today's challenging environment.

EFRAT NECHUSHTAI is an assistant professor in the School of Media and Public Affairs at the George Washington University.

$32.00 / £28.00 paper 978-0-231-22109-2
$130.00 / £109.00 cloth 978-0-231-22108-5

MAY 248 pages / 5.5" x 8.5" / 1 b&w illustration

JOURNALISM

REUTERS INSTITUTE GLOBAL JOURNALISM SERIES

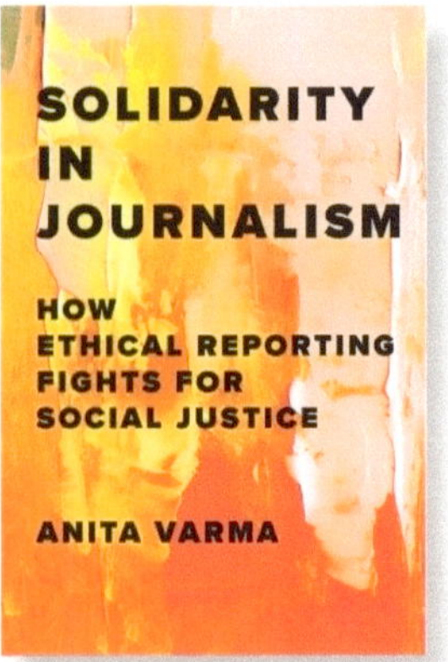

Solidarity in Journalism

How Ethical Reporting Fights for Social Justice

ANITA VARMA

"This book provides a road map for how journalists can better understand and share the lived experiences of marginalized people."

—Brian Ekdale, School of Journalism and Mass Communication, University of Iowa

Anita Varma offers a bold defense of reporting for social justice, showing what journalistic solidarity looks like in principle and in practice. She argues that solidarity is a longstanding yet unacknowledged journalistic norm that fosters truthful reporting when people's basic dignity is at stake. Varma illustrates ethical journalistic practices through case studies of local and national reporting on homelessness, housing instability, and the cost of living. Amid intense debate over the role of the media, this book makes an urgent case for solidarity in journalism as crucial for representing and addressing social division.

ANITA VARMA is an assistant professor in the School of Journalism and Media at the University of Texas at Austin. She also leads the Solidarity Journalism Initiative at the Center for Media Engagement, where she is a senior faculty research associate.

$30.00 / £25.00 paper 978-0-231-21547-3
$120.00 / £100.00 cloth 978-0-231-21546-6

APRIL 256 pages / 6" x 9" / 3 tables

JOURNALISM

The Tech-Media Hybrid

Google's News Ambition

QUN WANG

"A brilliant multimethod account of two decades of Google's technology-inspired attraction to news and its simultaneous struggles with journalism."

—Susan Keith, professor and associate dean, School of Communication and Information, Rutgers University

Qun Wang examines Google's engagement with news across more than two decades, tracing the company's complicated relationship with the news industry. She shows how what the company calls the "Google way" of experiencing news has exerted a profound influence on traditional media, and how Google's news ambitions, in turn, have been shaped by the global news industry's actions and reactions at every step. Shedding new light on the vast transformations of the past quarter century, this multimethod interdisciplinary book also offers insight into how the news environment might evolve in the era of AI.

QUN WANG, a former TV anchor, journalist, and news director, is an assistant professor in the Department of Communication and Media Studies at Fordham University.

$35.00 / £30.00 paper 978-0-231-20727-0
$140.00 / £115.00 cloth 978-0-231-20726-3

AVAILABLE NOW 304 pages / 5.5" x 8.5" / 12 b&w images

JOURNALISM

Making Statistics Work

Information Theory and Bayesian Inference

DUNCAN K. FOLEY AND ELLIS SCHARFENAKER

Conventional "frequentist" methods that dominate the field of statistics are generally inconsistent and liable to catastrophic failure in some contexts. *Making Statistics Work* presents a synthesis of information theory and Bayesian inference that addresses these fundamental problems. It provides a consistent, powerful, and flexible framework for data inference based on rigorous logic derived from first principles, allowing for new approaches to many of the unresolved questions of statistics.

DUNCAN K. FOLEY is the Leo Model Professor Emeritus of Economics at the New School for Social Research and external professor at the Santa Fe Institute. He is the author of *Understanding Capital: Marx's Economic Theory* (1986) and *Adam's Fallacy: A Guide to Economic Theology* (2006) and coauthor of *Growth and Distribution* (second edition, 2019), among other books.

ELLIS SCHARFENAKER is an associate professor of economics at the University of Utah. His research integrates Bayesian inference, information theory, and political economy to study industrial dynamics and income distribution.

$35.00 / £30.00 paper 978-0-231-22204-4
$140.00 / £117.00 cloth 978-0-231-22203-7

JULY 328 pages / 6.125" x 9.25" / 71 figures, 7 tables

STATISTICS / ECONOMICS

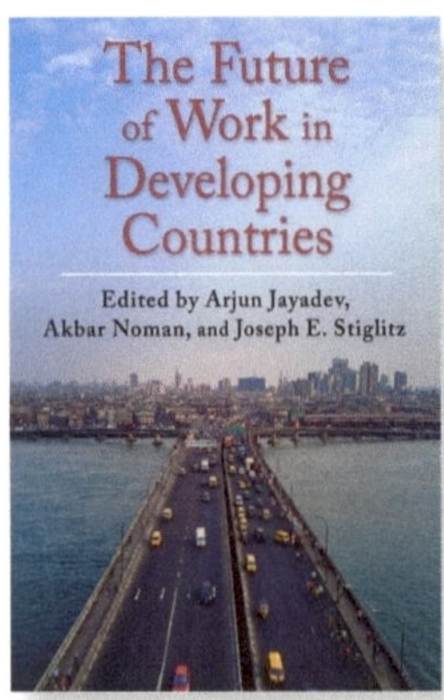

The Future of Work in Developing Countries

ARJUN JAYADEV, AKBAR NOMAN, AND JOSEPH E. STIGLITZ, EDITORS

"This excellent set of studies provides a clear, compelling set of analyses to help us understand what is clearly one of the 'wicked problems' of our times and a mapping of possible pathways to solve it."

—Jayati Ghosh, University of Massachusetts Amherst

Bringing together leading international scholars, this book examines the employment challenge in low- and middle-income countries from multiple perspectives. It demonstrates that employment creation is not an automatic byproduct of growth but a political and institutional project.

ARJUN JAYADEV is professor of economics and director of the Centre for the Study of the Indian Economy at Azim Premji University, Bangalore.

AKBAR NOMAN is senior fellow at the Initiative for Policy Dialogue and adjunct professor at the School of International and Public Affairs at Columbia University.

JOSEPH E. STIGLITZ, a recipient of the Nobel Memorial Prize in Economic Sciences, is University Professor and founding president of the Initiative for Policy Dialogue at Columbia University.

$75.00 / £62.00 cloth 978-0-231-22033-0
MARCH 480 pages / 6" x 9" / 189 b&w figures, 26 tables
ECONOMICS
INITIATIVE FOR POLICY DIALOGUE AT COLUMBIA: CHALLENGES IN DEVELOPMENT AND GLOBALIZATION

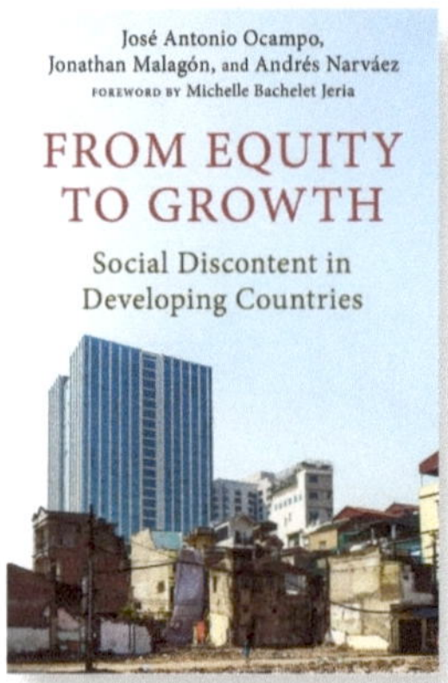

From Equity to Growth

Social Discontent in Developing Countries

JOSÉ ANTONIO OCAMPO, JONATHAN MALAGÓN, AND ANDRÉS NARVÁEZ

Foreword by Michelle Bachelet Jeria

"Timely and insightful."

—Mariana Mazzucato, University College London

This book presents specific policy choices that can reconcile social demands with macroeconomic stability, providing a road map to escape the middle-income trap without sacrificing fairness.

JOSÉ ANTONIO OCAMPO is a professor of professional practice at Columbia University's School of International and Public Affairs. He previously served as United Nations undersecretary general for economic and social affairs and minister of finance of Colombia.

JONATHAN MALAGÓN is the president and CEO of the Colombian Banking and Financial Institutions Association (Asobancaria) and an adjunct associate professor at Columbia University's School of International and Public Affairs.

ANDRÉS NARVÁEZ is the director of economics at PRIME Business School in Bogotá and a professor of microeconomics at the National University of Colombia.

MICHELLE BACHELET JERIA is the former president of Chile and former United Nations high commissioner for human rights.

$50.00 / £42.00 cloth 978-0-231-22291-4
JUNE 248 pages / 6" x 9" / 81 b&w figures, 4 tables
ECONOMICS
INITIATIVE FOR POLICY DIALOGUE AT COLUMBIA: CHALLENGES IN DEVELOPMENT AND GLOBALIZATION

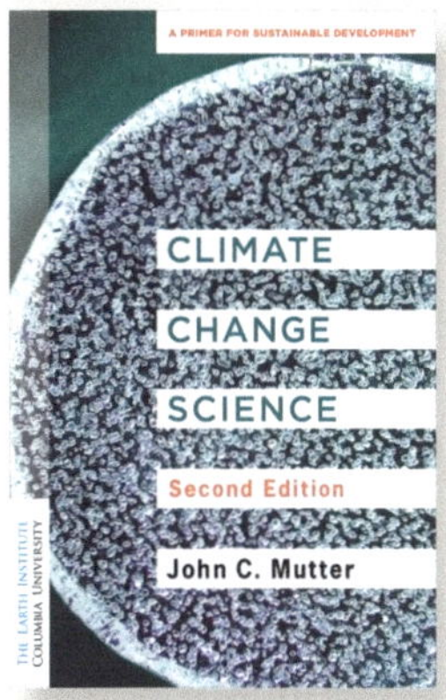

Climate Change Science

A Primer for Sustainable Development

Second edition

JOHN C. MUTTER

This book is a primer on the fundamental science of climate change and climate prediction, now updated to reflect the latest research. John C. Mutter gives a just-the-facts overview of how the climate system functions and what we know about why changes occur. This second edition incorporates updates including the most recent IPCC Assessment Report, adding discussion of attribution science—the ability to determine the extent to which extreme weather was the result of climate change—and a new chapter on geoengineering.

JOHN C. MUTTER is a professor at Columbia University with appointments in the Department of Earth and Environmental Sciences and in the School of International and Public Affairs as well as a faculty member of the Columbia Earth Institute. He is the author of *The Disaster Profiteers: How Natural Disasters Make the Rich Richer and the Poor Even Poorer* (2015) and coauthor of *Disasters and Development: An Earth Institute Sustainability Primer* (Columbia, 2025).

$20.00 / £16.99 paper 978-0-231-22047-7
$80.00 / £68.00 cloth 978-0-231-22046-0

MAY 240 pages / 5.5" x 8.5" / 95 figures

SCIENCE / CLIMATE CHANGE

COLUMBIA UNIVERSITY EARTH INSTITUTE SUSTAINABILITY PRIMERS

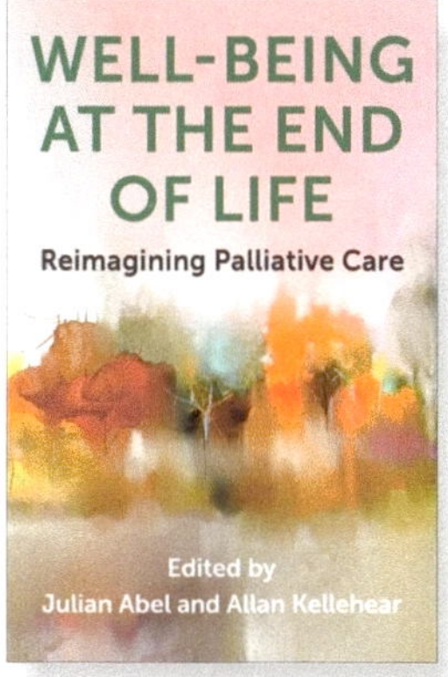

Well-Being at the End of Life

Reimagining Palliative Care

JULIAN ABEL AND ALLAN KELLEHEAR, EDITORS

"Well-written, accessible, and inspiring. This book will be of immense value to palliative care professionals and to others who work with aged populations."

—Ellen L. Idler, editor of *Religion as a Social Determinant of Public Health*

This state-of-the-field book argues that palliative care has drifted away from its transformative goals—and shows what to do about it. Bringing together leading international scholars and practitioners, *Well-Being at the End of Life* calls for a paradigm shift in the values and priorities of palliative care to emphasize the importance of community to personal well-being.

JULIAN ABEL is a palliative care physician and visiting professor at Northumbria University.

ALLAN KELLEHEAR is professor of end-of-life care at Northumbria University.

ABEL and **KELLEHEAR** are cofounders of Compassionate Communities UK and coeditors of the *Oxford Textbook of Public Health Palliative Care* (2022).

$32.00 / £25.00 paper 978-0-231-21628-9
$130.00 / £100.00 cloth 978-0-231-21627-2

MAY 240 pages / 6" x 9" / 6 b&w illustrations

SOCIAL WORK

END-OF-LIFE CARE: A SERIES

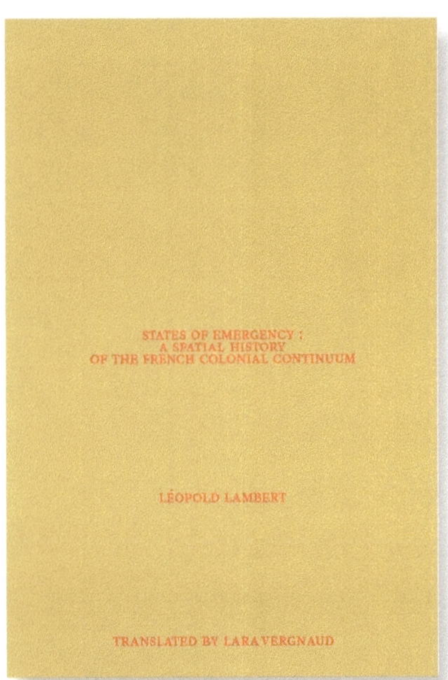

States of Emergency

A Spatial History of the French Colonial Continuum

LÉOPOLD LAMBERT

Translated by Lara Vergnaud

Foreword by Zoé Samudzi

States of Emergency navigates the temporal and spatial dimensions of France's states of emergency across three colonial space-times: the Algerian Revolution (1954–1962), the Kanak Insurrection (1984–1988), and the French banlieues riots (2005) and their fallout (2015–). In recounting the mechanics of this counterrevolutionary legal framework across multiple geographies—extending and fortifying key anticolonial solidarities past, present, and future—this book reads the state of emergency not as an exception but as a heightened form of everyday colonial state violence.

Contrasting the architecture of sites like "regroupement" camps in Algeria, the white settler city of Nouméa, and the police stations of Paris's suburbs with that of Algiers's Casbah, Kanaky's tribes, and Paris's banlieues, *States of Emergency* narrates the bureaucracies and protocols that continue to enable and underwrite the far-reaching violence of this legal measure as well as the anticolonial and antiracist resistance brought against it. The book offers a guide and a method for making the colonial continuum legible across contexts and for spatializing the many actors, agents, immigrants, and revolutionaries working both for and against the shared project of liberation.

Tribute in Algiers memorializing the October 17, 1961 Paris massacre. Photograph taken July 2018. Courtesy of the author.

LÉOPOLD LAMBERT is editor in chief of *The Funambulist*. He is a trained architect as well as the author of four books that examine the inherent violence of architecture on bodies and its political instrumentalization at various scales and in various geographical contexts, in particular Palestine.

LARA VERGNAUD has translated more than twenty books, including novels by Fatima Daas, Mohamed Leftah, Mohamed Mbougar Sarr, and Zahia Rahmani.

ZOÉ SAMUDZI is a postdoctoral scholar in African American and Africana studies at the Ohio State University.

$23.00* / £18.99 paper 978-1-941332-87-0

FEBRUARY 368 pages / 5.5" x 8" / 45 b&w photos and 10 maps

ARCHITECTURE

Material Variance

LOLA BEN-ALON, EDITOR

Raw building materials are inherently variable. This variability shapes global supply chains, labor relations, infrastructure, and trade networks. Yet within the context of building design, materials are often treated as static commodities. *Material Variance* resists this perception, unfolding instead a framework for designing through and with living matter that is uncertain, messy, and dynamic. The book insists on materials not as passive inputs but as unruly agents, shaped by and shaping the political, ecological, and cultural processes around them.

Convening material researchers, building scientists, architects, and artists, *Material Variance* aims to collectively expand architecture and design's material lexicon and unsettle its disciplinary boundaries. The book interrogates the assumptions of refinement, standardization, and technocratic control to advance alternative fabrication practices, alchemical processes, and methods for working with indeterminate matter. From poetic field recordings to scientific analyses, the book opens up a space for thinking across theory and practice, across geological particles and living species, and across various scales, forms, and practices.

Material Variance features three distinct covers, each one printed with a unique matrix, ink, paper stock, and tip-in, extending the notion of variance to the production of the object itself.

LOLA BEN-ALON is a material designer, engineer, and scholar of architectural technology. She is assistant professor at Columbia University's Graduate School of Architecture, Planning, and Preservation, where she directs the Natural Materials Lab and the Building Technology curriculum. Her research examines raw earth- and plant-based materials through design experimentation, fabrication, and environmental life cycle studies.

ANDRÉS JAQUE is dean and professor of Columbia University's Graduate School of Architecture, Planning, and Preservation and founder of the New York- and Madrid-based architecture practice Office for Political Innovation.

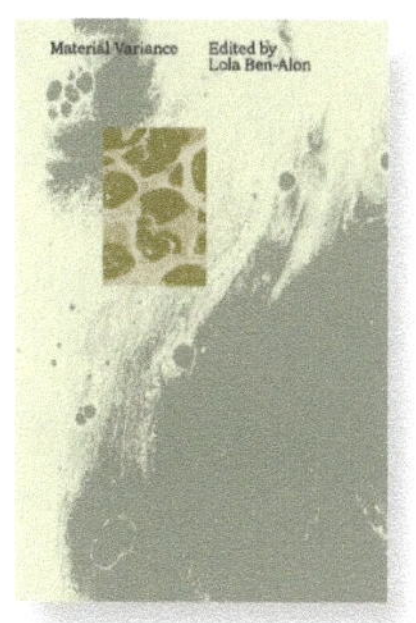

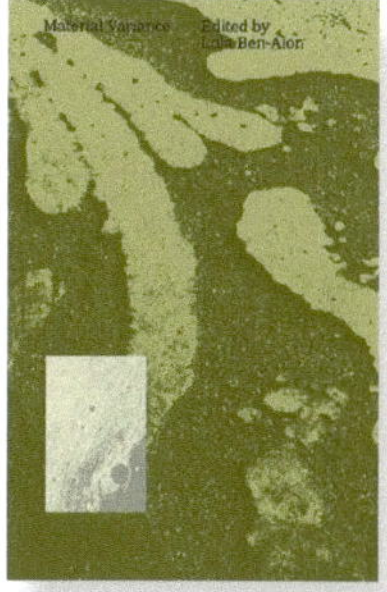

CONTRIBUTORS:

David Benjamin • Ethan Bourdeau • Olga Beatrice Carcassi • Caitlin Charlet • Felecia Davis • Andrés Jaque • Leslie Lok • Mae-ling Lokko • Claudia Mareis • Adam Marcus • V. Mitch McEwen • Ruth Morrow • Jorge Otero-Pailos • Ronald Rael • Jonsara Ruth • Laia Mogas-Soldevila

$28.00* / £22.00 paper 978-1-941332-86-3

FEBRUARY 300 pages / 5.5" x 8.5" / 157 color images and 30 figures

ARCHITECTURE

Building Postcarbon Futures
Land, Justice, and Energy Transitions
Billy Fleming

Building Postcarbon Futures

Land, Justice, and Energy Transitions

BILLY FLEMING

What would a postcarbon future look like? How would a more just, decarbonized world require us to change the way we live? What would it take to build this world? These questions lie at the heart of *Building Postcarbon Futures.*

This book offers a comprehensive account of the myriad ways in which people are transforming their social, ecological, and economic systems to create more just, beautiful places in response to the climate crisis. With contributions from more than a dozen leading scholars, *Building Postcarbon Futures* takes readers through thirty exemplary works of climate justice spanning forty-three countries and six continents. Together, these illustrated case studies foreground the overlooked tactics, strategies, and modes of practice being employed, often by marginalized peoples, to build a more just, decarbonized world—from Cuba to Kiribati.

Building Postcarbon Futures is both a celebration of action underway and a challenge to those tasked with bringing new works of climate justice into the built and natural environments—the planners, designers, policy makers, and activists pushing this planet toward a future of collective flourishing.

"A vigorous challenge to the stultified imagination of contemporary climate policy and design."

—Nikil Saval, Pennsylvania state senator and contributing editor of *n+1*

"A horizon of hope and a tour de force that is a must-read for urban studies and social justice scholars and practitioners."

—Ananya Roy, Meyer and Renee Luskin Chair in Inequality and Democracy, University of California, Los Angeles

"This book puts the earth, the land, and the spaces we all share at the center of the climate crisis, precisely where they belong."

—Julian Brave NoiseCat, author of *We Survived the Night* and director of *Sugarcane*

BILLY FLEMING is cofounder and strategic codirector of the Climate and Community Institute and assistant professor of landscape architecture at Temple University's Tyler School of Art and Architecture. Fleming is coeditor of *Design with Nature Now* (Lincoln Institute of Land Policy, 2019) and *A Blueprint for Coastal Adaptation: Uniting Design, Economics, and Policy* (2021).

CONTRIBUTORS:

Catherine de Almeida • Gianpaolo Baiocchi • Eliza Breder • Holly Jean Buck • Daniel Aldana Cohen • Keller Easterling • Kian Goh • Rob Holmes • Leah Kahler • Reinhold Martin • Danielle Rivera • Douglas Robb • Akira Drake Rodriguez • Matthew Seibert • Aaryaman "Sunny" Singhal • Abby Spinak • Charles Waldheim

$45.00 / £38.00 paper 978-1-55844-456-0

APRIL 550 pages / 8" x 10" / Color photos, maps, and figures throughout

CLIMATE CHANGE / SOCIAL JUSTICE

Planning in a Polycrisis

Equitable Urban Strategies for a Changing Climate

EMILIA OSCILOWICZ, JAMES J. T. CONNOLLY, AND ISABELLE ANGUELOVSKI

The intersecting challenges of climate change, housing affordability, and economic inequality are creating fierce competition for resources, attention, time, and capacity as communities respond to a mounting polycrisis. This report outlines strategies for addressing these vexing issues, drawing on research including interviews with planners and policy makers in five North American cities: Boston, Denver, Portland, Vancouver, and Washington, DC. It offers actionable insights to help cities move from fragmented planning efforts toward long-term, justice-centered urban transformation, proposing an equitable climate urbanism framework that emphasizes cross-sector collaboration, resilient housing, place-based adaptation, and inclusive community engagement. By marrying climate action with housing initiatives and economic development, this framework can yield more climate-friendly, affordable homes while cultivating the agency, participation, and engagement of historically marginalized communities. *Planning in a Polycrisis* shows the way toward more resilient, affordable, and inclusive communities.

EMILIA OSCILOWICZ is a doctoral student at the Universitat Autònoma de Barcelona and the University of Colorado Denver.

JAMES J. T. CONNOLLY is an associate professor of community and regional planning at the University of British Columbia.

ISABELLE ANGUELOVSKI is an ICREA Research Professor at the Universitat Autònoma de Barcelona.

All authors are affiliated with the Barcelona Laboratory for Urban Environmental Justice and Sustainability at the Institute of Environmental Sciences and Technology within the Universitat Autònoma de Barcelona.

"I think we need to get more sophisticated and move beyond the idea of green gentrification and say, 'What are the solutions here?'"

—municipal climate action planner, Denver

$20.00 / £16.99 paper 978-1-55844-476-8

MARCH 80 pages / 8″ x 10″ / Color photos and figures throughout

LAND USE AND PLANNING / SOCIAL JUSTICE

POLICY FOCUS REPORTS

Hitchcock Annual

SIDNEY GOTTLIEB, EDITOR

The *Hitchcock Annual* seeks to publish the best in critical and scholarly essays in Hitchcock studies. We welcome articles from a wide variety of theoretical, critical, and historical perspectives on the life, work, and influence of Alfred Hitchcock.

All back issues of the *Hitchcock Annual* are available through Columbia University Press, as is *The Hitchcock Annual Anthology: Selected Essays from Volumes 10–15*, edited by Sidney Gottlieb and Richard Allen (2009, $26.00 paper 978-1-905673-95-4/ $80.00 cloth 978-1-905673-96-1).

NOW AVAILABLE

Hitchcock Annual

Volume 28

SIDNEY GOTTLIEB, EDITOR

Hitchcock Annual volume 28 contains essays on Hitchcock's Catholicism, the reception of *I Confess* in France, *Murder!* and *Mary*, *Rebecca* and the Gothic, O in *North by Northwest*, and Annie Hayworth in *The Birds*. Detailed review essays cover recent books on selected shots in Hitchcock, Hitchcock and noir, and his use of storyboards.

SIDNEY GOTTLIEB is professor of communication and media arts at Sacred Heart University.

$26.00 / £22.00 paper 978-0-231-22068-2
AVAILABLE NOW 225 pages / 5.5" x 8.5" / illustrations throughout
FILM STUDIES

FORTHCOMING

Hitchcock Annual

Volume 29

SIDNEY GOTTLIEB, EDITOR

Hitchcock Annual volume 29 is due out in summer 2026. Planned contents include essays on *I Confess*, Catholic contexts for Hitchcock's visuality, and Hitchcock as an entertainer, as well as reviews of recent critical books on Hitchcock.

SIDNEY GOTTLIEB is professor of communication and media arts at Sacred Heart University.

$26.00 / £22.00 paper 978-0-231-22386-7
AUGUST 160 pages / 5.5" x 8.5" / illustrations throughout
FILM STUDIES

The **ERIS Dialogues** series gathers real and imagined conversations between writers, artists, and philosophers whose exchanges illuminate the life of the mind. Each volume stages an encounter in which ideas are tested, voices collide, and thought takes dramatic form.

The Stories We Bring Back

Margaret Atwood on Myth, Mortality, and the Art of Writing

MARGARET ATWOOD AND HARIS VLAVIANOS

In this wide-ranging and characteristically fearless exchange, Margaret Atwood sits down in Athens with the poet and philosopher Haris Vlavianos to reflect on myth, politics, mortality, and the creative imagination. From Homer to *The Handmaid's Tale*, from Tiresias to Trump, their conversation traces the long arc between ancient story and present crisis. With sardonic humor and precision, Atwood revisits her own work through the eyes of myth: Penelope and her maids, sirens and shapeshifters, prophets and tyrants. Each theme circles the archetypal journey into darkness and return—the descent that art demands and the question it leaves us with: What stories survive, and what do we bring back from the descent?

As the dialogue unfolds, Atwood speaks with unusual intimacy about the practice of writing—its rituals and terrors, its moral weight, its comic absurdities. The result is both public conversation and private meditation, a spirited encounter between two minds steeped in literature and alive to the political urgencies of our time. At once erudite and mischievous, *The Stories We Bring Back* reveals Atwood at her most lucid and unguarded.

"Writers descend to the underworld and what they bring back is a story. It's darkness and then illumination. And no matter how gloomy the content, every act of writing is an act of optimism."

—from *The Stories We Bring Back*

MARGARET ATWOOD is the author of more than fifty books of fiction, poetry, and essays, including *The Handmaid's Tale*, *The Testaments*, *Oryx and Crake*, and *Burning Questions*. She has received the Booker Prize, the PEN Pinter Prize, the Franz Kafka Prize, and the Dayton Literary Peace Prize.

HARIS VLAVIANOS is professor of history, political theory, and history of ideas at the American College of Greece and editor of the literary journal *Poetics*. He is the author of more than a dozen collections of poetry and essays and has translated T. S. Eliot, Ezra Pound, Wallace Stevens, Anne Carson, and William Blake into Greek.

$19.99* / £16.99 paper 978-1-967751-78-5
JANUARY 72 pages / 4.25" x 7.67"
LITERARY STUDIES

ART INTERNATIONAL

Michael Peppiatt Jill Lloyd

Art International

Anthology of Postwar Art Writing

MICHAEL PEPPIATT AND JILL LLOYD, EDITORS

For more than three decades, *Art International* was the beating heart of the postwar art world—a magazine where artists and critics met as equals, ideas crossed oceans, and modern art found its global voice. Founded in Zurich in 1959 by the maverick American James Fitzsimmons, it became the essential forum for the era's sharpest minds: Clement Greenberg, Harold Rosenberg, Lucy Lippard, Rosalind Krauss, Michael Fried, John Berger, Jacques Derrida, and Gilles Deleuze. Here the great debates of modernism and its aftermath played out, from abstract expressionism to pop, minimalism to conceptualism, with artists such as Bacon, Judd, Motherwell, and Kiefer speaking directly from its pages.

This definitive anthology, edited by *Art International*'s final editors, Michael Peppiatt and Jill Lloyd, gathers the magazine's most original and influential writing—along with artists' manifestos, correspondence, and rare critical texts unseen for decades. Lavishly illustrated with archival material, covers, and artworks, it offers a vivid panorama of art's most transformative period and the critics who made sense of it.

MICHAEL PEPPIATT was the arts editor at *Réalités* and *Le Monde* in Paris. In 1985 he bought *Art International*. Peppiatt is the author of a dozen books, including the acclaimed memoir *Francis Bacon in Your Blood* and *Only Too Much Is Enough: Francis Bacon in His Own Words* (2021).

JILL LLOYD is an art historian and curator. She is the author of *German Expressionism: Primitivism and Modernity* and *The Undiscovered Expressionist: A Life of Marie-Louise Von Motesiczky*. She has curated major exhibitions and currently serves as a trustee at the Neue Galerie New York.

$39.99* / £35.00 paper 978-1-967751-77-8

MAY 440 pages / 8" x 10" / 75 color illustrations

ART

Collected Writings

Essays, Poems, Interviews

Volume I: The Antitheatrical Imperative and Other Essays

Volume II: The Edge of the Table: Prose Poems

Volume III: Exit Interviews

MICHAEL FRIED

This collection brings together three interrelated volumes by the renowned writer and thinker Michael Fried. In studies of painters as varied as Caravaggio, Fragonard, and Matisse, Fried has transformed how we understand artistic form and technique, and his insightful literary-critical work has been enriched by his practice as a highly accomplished poet. Imbued with the distinctive combination of perceptiveness, imagination, and analytical rigor that he has displayed throughout his career, *Collected Writings* also serves as a personal record of Fried's intellectual and critical formation.

The first volume, *The Antitheatrical Imperative and Other Essays*, ranges in topic from Manet to Pollock. The second volume, *The Edge of the Table*, is a collection of exquisitely constructed prose poems accompanied by photographs by James Welling. The third volume, *Exit Interviews*, is an autobiographical text that retraces the development of the arguments and ideas that informed Fried's groundbreaking works while paying close attention to both the personal and institutional contexts of intellectual labor.

MICHAEL FRIED is professor emeritus of the humanities at Johns Hopkins University. He is the author of numerous scholarly works—most recently *What Was Literary Impressionism?*; *Painting with Demons: The Art of Gerolamo Savoldo*; and *French Suite: A Book of Essays*—and four volumes of poetry.

MICHAEL FRIED
COLLECTED WRITINGS
ESSAYS, POEMS, INTERVIEWS

"Fried is a poet of the utmost integrity."

—J. M. Coetzee

"No one sees paintings better than Michael Fried or thinks as persistently or with such philosophical depth about such seeing, about the very possibility of pictorial meaning."

—Robert B. Pippin

$60.00* / £50.00 paper 978-1-91680976-5

FEBRUARY 1250 pages / 4.33" x 6.9" / 53 color illustrations

ART / LITERATURE / ESSAYS

VOLUME I:

$19.99* / £16.99 paper 978-1-916809-22-2

FEBRUARY 548 pages / 4.33" x 6.9" / 53 color illustrations

VOLUME II:

$19.99* / £16.99 paper 978-1-916809-21-5

FEBRUARY 384 pages / 4.33" x 6.9" / 10 b&w illustrations

VOLUME III:

$19.99* / £16.99 paper 978-1-916809-09-3

FEBRUARY 318 pages / 4.33" x 6.9"

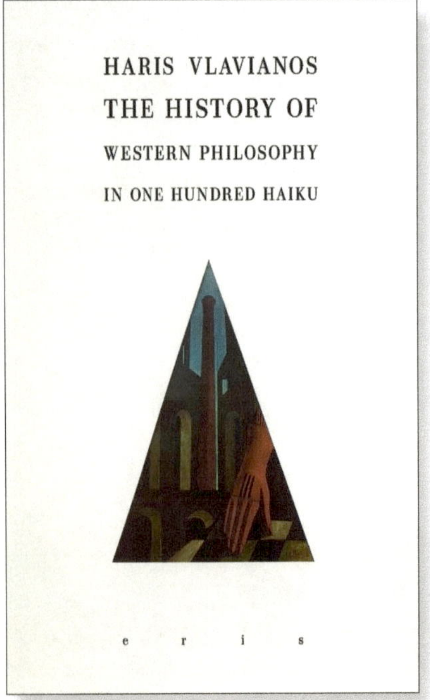

The History of Western Philosophy in 100 Haiku

HARIS VLAVIANOS

Translated by Peter Mackridge

In this audacious pocket history, the poet Haris Vlavianos compresses Western philosophy from Thales to Nussbaum into 100 razor-sharp haikus. Plato gets a cave with "all mod cons." Kant boots up a "laptop mind." Wittgenstein tries to coax a fly from its bottle. It's Russell meets Bashō, Socrates with a punchline—and beneath the wit, real argument and insight. Rendered into live, witty English by Peter Mackridge, *The History of Western Philosophy in 100 Haiku* is for anyone who likes big ideas distilled to their brightest essence.

HARIS VLAVIANOS is professor of history, political theory, and history of ideas at the American College of Greece and editor of the literary journal *Poetics*. He is the author of more than a dozen collections of poetry and essays and has translated T. S. Eliot, Ezra Pound, Wallace Stevens, Anne Carson, and William Blake into Greek.

PETER MACKRIDGE is emeritus professor of modern Greek at the University of Oxford and a visiting professor at King's College London.

13. PLATO

The Republic

That cave is fitted
with all mod cons. It even
has television!

58. FRIEDRICH NIETZSCHE

Twilight of the Idols

My work has driven
me mad—hammering away
at false idols.

93. BERNARD WILLIAMS

Ethics and the Limits of Philosophy

You've wasted a lot
of time in theorizing.
Get yourself a life.

$19.99* / £16.99 paper 978-1-967751-80-8
MAY 126 pages / 4.25" x 6.87"
POETRY / PHILOSOPHY

Etymologies

And Other Rites

EFTHIMIS FILIPPOU

Translated by Kyriacos Karseras

In *Etymologies and Other Rites*, language, family, and fate are laid bare on the slab. Efthimis Filippou—acclaimed screenwriter of *Dogtooth*, *The Lobster*, and *The Killing of a Sacred Deer*—moves between lecture, cabaret, and liturgy with a poker face that leaves space for awe. His stage world is one of rituals disguised as bureaucracies, where saints and civil servants coexist, where grief becomes procedure, and humor, a form of prayer. Songs flare, knives appear, miracles are audited like minutes from a meeting. Taken together, these four works, *Etymologies* (a play), *Big and Small Ships* (a ritual performance), *Eau de Cologne* (a choral device), and *George* (a narrative), form a darkly luminous cycle about belief and substitution—of tongues, bodies, and meanings—played out between the sacred and the absurd.

EFTHIMIS FILIPPOU is a Greek writer, playwright, and screenwriter. He has gained broad international recognition through his collaboration with director Yorgos Lanthimos, cowriting the scripts for *Dogtooth*, *Alps*, *The Lobster*, *The Killing of a Sacred Deer*, and *Kinds of Kindness*.

$24.99* / £20.00 paper 978-1-967751-82-2

MARCH 176 pages / 5" x 8"

LITERATURE IN TRANSLATION

Homes of Hades

Photographs by Kleopatra Haritou

KLEOPATRA HARITOU

Homes of Hades is Kleopatra Haritou's haunting dialogue between the living and the dead—between Athens above and Athens below. Through her subversive lens, the marble thresholds of postwar apartment buildings become twin gates to the city's cemeteries; the entrances of the living echo the exits of the departed. The book presents 190 color photographs, each laid out in diptych spreads where one image depicts an Athenian apartment entrance and its facing pair a tombstone, shrine, or grave. What begins as an existential exploration unfolds as an unexpected portrait of modern Greece—from the ruins of antiquity to the neon glow of the Western present. In *Homes of Hades* (copublished with the Onassis Foundation), every ending is the next beginning.

KLEOPATRA HARITOU has exhibited widely in Greece and internationally, including the landmark solo show *Prosfygika* at the Benaki Museum and the public installation series *Acrobats*. She has received awards from Pentax, Leica, and Kodak.

$34.99* / £30.00 cloth 978-1-967751-98-3

FEBRUARY 208 pages / 9" x 11" / 190 color photographs

PHOTOGRAPHY

ERIS CRITICAL CENTURY SERIES

Critical Century gathers some of the most urgent and enduring works of the twentieth century—a time of fracture, experimentation, and radical thinking. These are texts from the edges of literature, philosophy, politics, and art, where form meets force and thinking becomes resistance. Essays, manifestos, notebooks, film scripts, city portraits—each one sharp, unsettling, and still very much alive: a library of modernism at its most combustible.

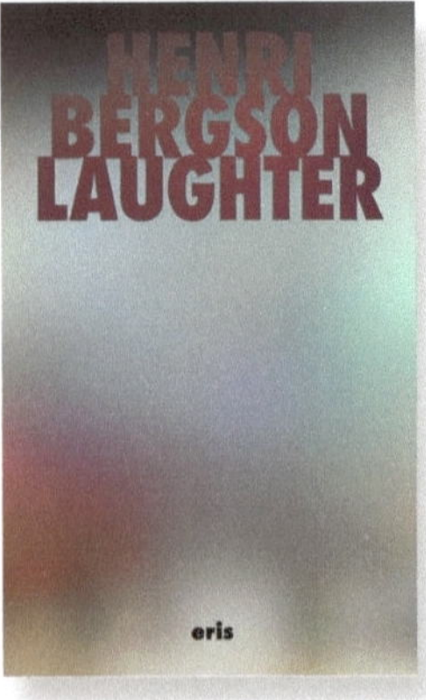

Laughter

An Essay on the Meaning of the Comic

New edition

HENRI BERGSON

Introduction by Simon Critchley

Afterword by Wyndham Lewis

In this classic 1900 essay, the philosopher Henri Bergson anatomizes the comic impulse with surgical clarity and lyrical wit. With a rejoinder essay by Wyndham Lewis and a new introduction by Simon Critchley, *Laughter* emerges as both a foundational text in aesthetics and a startlingly modern theory of humor—anticipating Freud, Chaplin, and memes alike.

HENRI BERGSON was one of the most influential philosophers of the twentieth century and winner of the Nobel Prize in Literature (1927). **SIMON CRITCHLEY** is the Hans Jonas Professor of Philosophy at the New School for Social Research. His many books include *Mysticism* and *I Want to Die, I Hate My Life* (ERIS, 2025). **WYNDHAM LEWIS** was a British novelist, painter, and polemicist.

$22.99* / £18.99 paper 978-1-967751-84-6

JANUARY 160 pages / 5.2" x 9.1"

PHILOSOPHY

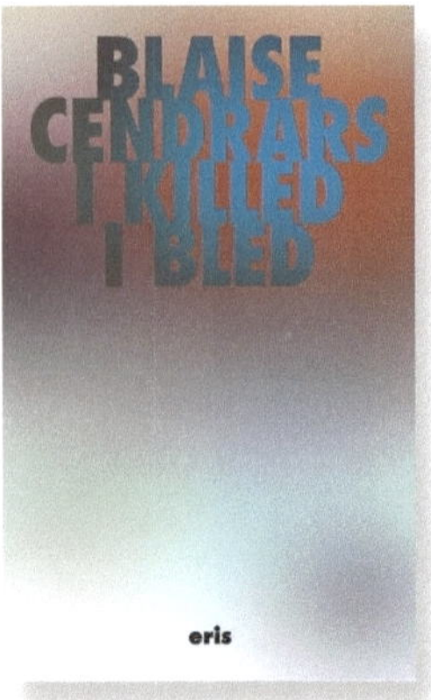

I Killed and I Bled

New edition

BLAISE CENDRARS

Blaise Cendrars enlisted in the French Foreign Legion in 1914 and in 1915 lost the lower half of his right arm—his writing hand. *I Killed* (1918) is Cendrars's first published account from the trenches. His shocking prose refuses theatrics. It anatomizes dehumanization—the drift from "we" to "I," the reduction of persons to numbers and parts, the obscene efficiency of industrial slaughter. *I Bled* (1938) looks back through hospitals and aftermaths. Framed here with a concise preface and notes, *I Killed and I Bled* is war writing that neither flatters nor absolves—language held against extinction.

BLAISE CENDRARS (1887–1961) was a Swiss French poet, novelist, editor, and tireless modernist. A volunteer in the French Foreign Legion during the First World War, he lost his right hand and taught himself to write left-handed. His books—*La prose du transsibérien, Moravagine, La main coupée*—made him one of the twentieth century's most intrepid and original voices.

$14.99* / £12.99 paper 978-1-967751-87-7

JANUARY 60 pages / 5.2" x 9.1"

LITERATURE IN TRANSLATION

ERIS GEMS

ERIS gems make available in the form of beautifully produced saddle-stitched booklets a series of outstanding short works of fiction and nonfiction.

On the Fragility of Life

NICK CAVE

$8.00* / £6.99 paper 978-1-967751-73-0

JANUARY 36 pages / 4.3" x 7.6"

MUSIC

Face to Face

CARL JUNG

$8.00* / £6.99 paper 978-1-967751-75-4

JANUARY 32 pages / 4.3" x 7.6"

PSYCHOLOGY

What Is Fear?

GIORGIO AGAMBEN

$8.00* / £6.99 paper 978-1-967751-50-1

AVAILABLE NOW 16 pages / 4.33" x 7.67"

PHILOSOPHY

From Protest to Politics

BAYARD RUSTIN

$8.00* / £6.99 paper 978-1-967751-96-9

JANUARY 12 pages / 4.3" x 7.6"

POLITICS

The Glow of the Dim

JUN'ICHIRŌ TANIZAKI

$8.00* / £6.99 paper 978-1-967751-47-1

AVAILABLE NOW 28 pages / 4.33" x 7.67"

LITERATURE IN TRANSLATION

Just a Little One

DOROTHY PARKER

$8.00* / £6.99 paper 978-1-967751-94-5

JANUARY 12 pages / 4.3" x 7.6"

LITERATURE

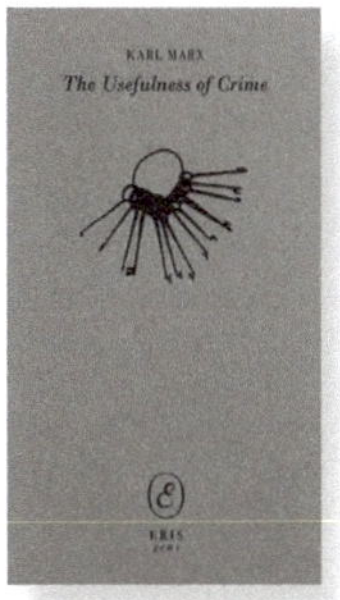

The Usefulness of Crime

KARL MARX

$8.00* / £6.99 paper 978-1-967751-52-5

AVAILABLE NOW 8 pages / 4.33" x 7.67"

PHILOSOPHY

The Signal-Man

CHARLES DICKENS

$8.00* / £6.99 paper 978-1-967751-90-7

JANUARY 20 pages / 4.3" x 7.6"

LITERATURE

Individualism and Conformism in the United States

JEAN-PAUL SARTRE

$8.00* / £6.99 paper 978-1-967751-92-1

JANUARY 32 pages / 4.3" x 7.6"

PHILOSOPHY

FOR SALE THROUGHOUT THE WORLD

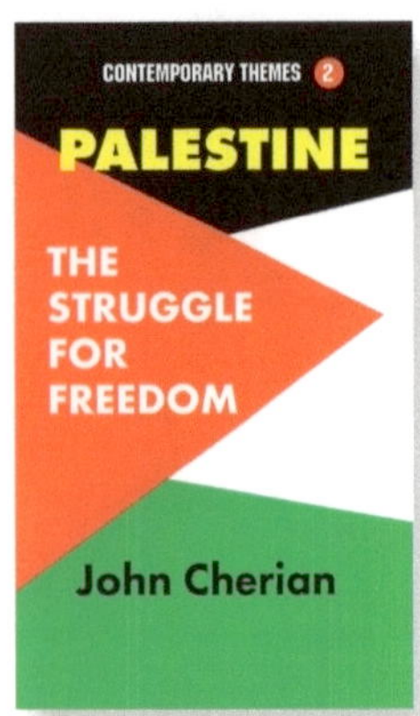

Palestine

The Struggle for Freedom

JOHN CHERIAN

This book explores the events leading to the current genocide in Gaza and far-right Jewish settler onslaught in the occupied West Bank. Beginning with the historical background to the establishment of Israel as a settler-colonial state, it examines key historical events since 1948, including the 1967 war, the Oslo Accords, the rise of Hamas, and internal Palestinian divisions in the 1990s. The book also critiques the international community's failure to hold Israel accountable for war crimes and highlights the role of US administrations in obstructing a two-state solution.

JOHN CHERIAN is a former international affairs correspondent for the magazine *Frontline*. He focused on issues relating to the Global South and covered the West Asian region extensively for more than three decades.

$12.00 / £9.99 paper 978-81-9793831-3
JUNE 124 pages / 4.5" x 7.5"'
POLITICS
CONTEMPORARY THEMES #2

Finance and Development

Essays Presented to C.P. Chandrasekhar

ROHIT AZAD, SURAJIT MAZUMDAR AND PARTHAPRATIM PAL, EDITORS

This edited volume celebrates the work of C. P. Chandrasekar, a leading economist from the Global South. True to his varied expertise, interests, and research, the essays here cover a wide array of issues, such as money and finance, industrial policy, climate finance, financialization, imperialism, and social reproduction. They also provide a roadmap beyond neoliberalism for the world in general and the Global South in particular. This volume should interest all who believe in a political and economic alternative to the current orthodox approach to economic theory and policy.

ROHIT AZAD is assistant professor at the Centre for Economic Studies and Planning, Jawaharlal Nehru University, New Delhi.

SURAJIT MAZUMDAR is professor at the Centre for Economic Studies and Planning, Jawaharlal Nehru University, New Delhi.

PARTHAPRATIM PAL is professor at the Indian Institute of Management, Calcutta.

$36.00 / £30.00 cloth 978-81-9793837-5
JUNE 208 pages / 6.25" x 9.5"
ECONOMICS

FOR SALE THROUGHOUT THE WORLD, EXCLUDING SOUTH ASIA

Subarnarekha

Ritwik Ghatak's Partition Quartet The Screenplays, volume 4

IRA BHASKAR, EDITOR

Translated by Shampa Banerjee

The concluding volume of the Partition Quartet Screenplays of Ritwik Ghatak, *Subarnarekha* is a devastating critique of the fallout of the partition. Set in postpartition Bengal, it chronicles the journey of refugee families as they attempt to settle down in a new land after surviving the worst bloodbath witnessed in the history of the subcontinent and the mass migration that followed. Ghatak's cinematic narrative, in the "critical melodramatic" form, acquires tremendous resonance through the use of music, myth, archetypes, and allegory to articulate a critique of modern civilization's destructive potential.

IRA BHASKAR retired as professor of cinema studies at Jawaharlal Nehru University, New Delhi. She is coeditor of *Bombay Cinema's Islamicate Histories* (2022).

SHAMPA BANERJEE is a literature scholar with a deep interest in cinema. She has worked on postproduction reconstructions and translations of film scripts, including Satyajit Ray's *Apu Trilogy*.

$16.00 / £12.99 paper 978-81-9793839-9

JUNE 128 pages / 6.25" x 9.5" / 50 b&w illustrations

FILM STUDIES

RITWIK GHATAK'S PARTITION QUARTET:THE SCREENPLAYS

Before My Memories Fade

P. Bhaskaran—Rebel, Poet, Lyricist, Filmmaker

P. BHASKARAN

Translated by Jyothi Unniraman

Between the covers of this book lie mnemonic snapshots of a towering figure in Malayalam poetry, song, and cinema, P. Bhaskaran. These recollections, translated from the Malayalam in his birth centenary year, trace his journey from boyhood through a revolutionary youth to his emergence as a luminous poetic voice. Woven through all his work is a profound humanism. He gave voice to the emotions of ordinary people in a language unmistakably their own, even as his vision helped shape the modern, democratic identity of the Malayali.

An initial translation was done by Jyoti Unniraman. This is a further translation, including some verse, by Sashi Kumar.

P. BHASKARAN (1924–2007) was a renowned poet, lyricist, and filmmaker of Kerala. He penned more than 3,000 songs for about 250 Malayalam films. He directed forty-four feature films and three documentaries, produced six feature films, and acted in several movies.

JYOTHI UNNIRAMAN retired as deputy director from the All India Management Association. She has published several translations and articles in Malayalam in popular magazines.

$30.00 / £25.00 paper 978-81-9937909-1

JUNE 200 pages / 6.25" x 9.5" / 20 b&w illustrations

MEMOIR

Spectral Conrad

AGNIESZKA ADAMOWICZ-POŚPIECH, EDITOR

This groundbreaking collection redefines Joseph Conrad's fiction through the innovative lens of spectrality studies, offering fresh perspectives that challenge and expand contemporary scholarly discourse. *Spectral Conrad* unites an array of international voices to dissect the haunting motifs, ghostly presences, and existential uncertainties woven into Conrad's iconic works. Through meticulous analysis of texts such as "Heart of Darkness," *Lord Jim*, *The Shadow-Line*, *Under Western Eyes*, *Victory*, "Prince Roman," "Freya of the Seven Isles," *Nostromo*, "Karain: A Memory," and "The Warrior's Soul," the volume illuminates Conrad's fascination with the spectral—from lingering traumas of colonialism to the ethical shadows of human ambition.

Drawing on frameworks as diverse as Plato's dialogues, Derrida's hauntology, Shakespearean tragedy, and cross-cultural literary traditions, the contributors—from universities in Greece, France, Japan, the United Kingdom, the United States, and Poland—forge a dynamic, globally informed critique. Their interdisciplinary approach reveals how spectrality shapes Conrad's narratives, transforming his fiction into a mirror for modern anxieties about identity, memory, and the unresolved legacies of history. Rich in theoretical rigor yet accessible in style, *Spectral Conrad* bridges academic depth with engaging analysis, making it an indispensable resource for students and scholars of modernism, postcolonial studies, and Gothic literature. This volume not only revitalizes Conrad's oeuvre but also reimagines spectrality as a vital critical tool.

The book is volume 34 of the series Conrad: Eastern and Western Perspectives, edited by Wiesław Krajka.

AGNIESZKA ADAMOWICZ-POŚPIECH is professor at the University of Silesia in Katowice, Poland, and president of the Joseph Conrad Society, Poland. She is the author of *Adaptations of Joseph Conrad's Life and Works in Contemporary Culture* (2022) and *Travels with Conrad* (2016) and editor of *The Resonance of Joseph Conrad in Contemporary Culture* (2025), among others. She is on the editorial boards of *The Conradian*, *Conradiana*, and the *Yearbook of Conrad Studies*. She is also a trustee of the Joseph Conrad Society of America.

TABLE OF CONTENTS:

$80.00 / £68.00 e-book 978-83-227-9931-4

DECEMBER 275 pages

LITERARY STUDIES

CONRAD: EASTERN AND WESTERN PERSPECTIVES

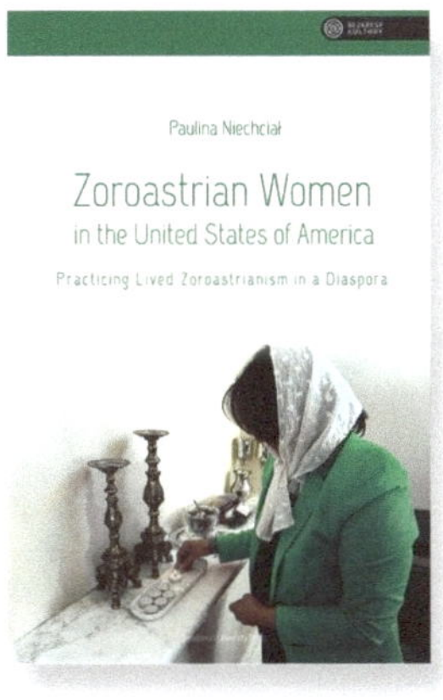

Zoroastrian Women in the United States of America

Practicing Lived Zoroastrianism in a Diaspora

PAULINA NIECHCIAŁ

This book examines how ancient Zoroastrianism is practiced in the United States diaspora and how it has evolved, moving beyond the dominant male perspective to focus on women. Zoroastrianism in their everyday experiences is more than a religion: it is a spiritual path, an ethnic tradition, and a cultural identity. Richly illustrated with the narratives of generations of Iranian and Parsi immigrants as well as photos, this book gives a sense of the diversity of Zoroastrian life across the United States. It not only broadens the picture of the ethnoreligious landscape of the country but also highlights the role of social practice theory in the study of religion, demonstrating how it applies to qualitative field research.

PAULINA NIECHCIAŁ is an assistant professor at the Center for Comparative Civilization Studies at the Jagiellonian University in Krakow, Poland. She is the author of *Zoroastrian Minority in Modern Tehran: On Collective Identity in the Context of Shi'a Domination* (2013).

$50.00 / £42.00 paper 978-83-233-5520-5
$49.99 / £42.00 Web PDF 978-83-233-7687-3
$49.99 / £42.00 EPUB 978-83-233-7688-0

AUGUST 378 pages / 6" x 9" / 1 color & 1 b&w map, 1 b&w chart, 52 color photos, 1 b&w figure

RELIGION

THE VASTNESS OF CULTURE

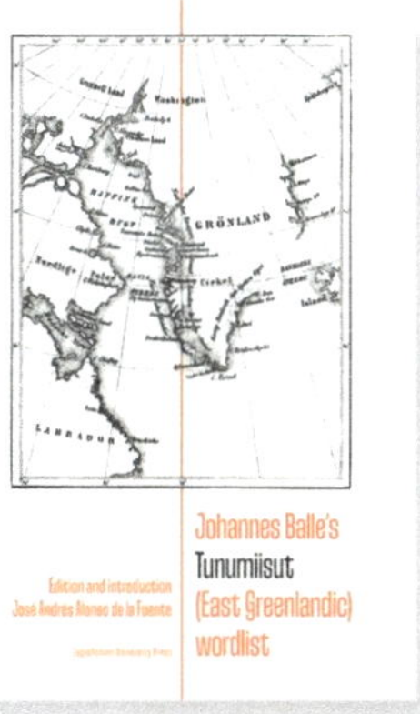

Johannes Balle's Tunumiisut (East Greenlandic) Wordlist

EDITED WITH AN INTRODUCTION BY JOSÉ ANDRÉS ALONSO DE LA FUENTE

This book examines the Tunumiisut (East Greenlandic) wordlist gathered by Johannes Balle (1889–1965) some time in the first half of the twentieth century. This little-known vocabulary, which includes equivalents in Kalaallisut (West Greenlandic) and translations into Danish, offers valuable data from a time when information on Greenlandic dialects was scarce and difficult to obtain. The book describes the historical context of Johannes Balle's life and the peculiarities of the linguistic data as presented in the wordlist. The main part of the study is the Tunumiisut wordlist rearranged according to English keywords for historical and comparative purposes. Extensive indexes arranged in the more traditional alphabetical order allow the reader to navigate easily through Tunumiisut, Kalaallisut, Proto-Inuit-Yupik, and Proto-Inuit reconstructions, all of them cross-referenced with the English keywords.

JOSÉ ANDRÉS ALONSO DE LA FUENTE is associate professor at the Institute of Linguistics, Translation Studies, and Hungarian Studies of the Jagiellonian University in Kraków.

$35.00 / £30.00 paper 978-83-233-5483-3

NOVEMBER 220 pages / 6.69" x 9.61" / 1 b&w map, 1 b&w photo, 6 b&w figures

LINGUISTICS

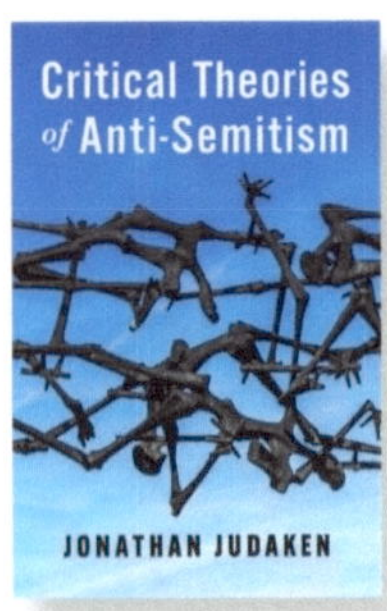

Critical Theories of Anti-Semitism

JONATHAN JUDAKEN

Winner, 2025 Dorothy Rosenberg Prize in Jewish Diaspora History, American Historical Association

$35.00 / £30.00 paper 978-0-231-21293-9

2024 RELIGION

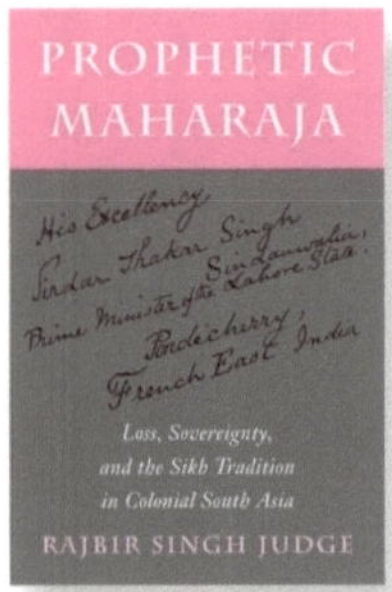

Prophetic Maharaja

RAJBIR SINGH JUDGE

Winner, 2025 Best First Book in the History of Religions, American Academy of Religion

Finalist, 2025 Book Award in Analytical-Descriptive Studies, American Academy of Religion

$35.00 / £30.00 paper 978-0-231-21449-0

2024 RELIGION

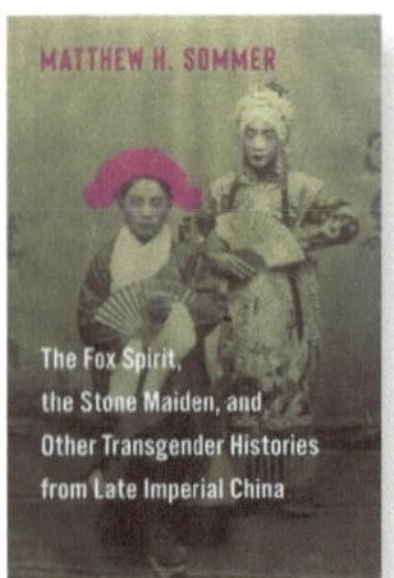

The Fox Spirit, the Stone Maiden, and Other Transgender Histories from Late Imperial China

MATTHEW H. SOMMER

Winner, 2025 John K. Fairbank Prize, American Historical Association

Winner, 2025 Peter Gonville Stein Book Award, American Society for Legal History

$30.00 / £25.00 paper 978-0-231-21413-1

2024 HISTORY

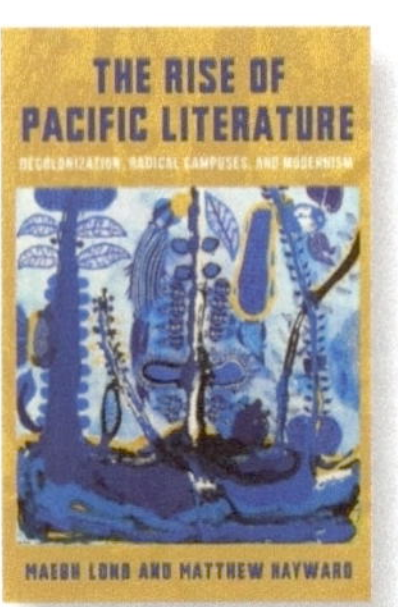

The Rise of Pacific Literature

MAEBH LONG AND MATTHEW HAYWARD

Winner, 2025 MSA Book Prize, Modernist Studies Association

$35.00 / £30.00 paper 978-0-231-21745-3

2024 LITERARY STUDIES

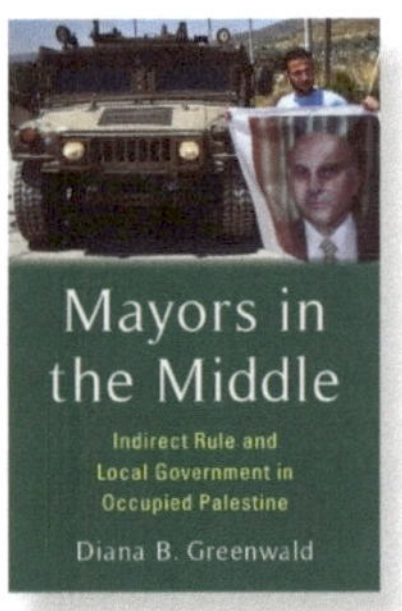

Mayors in the Middle

DIANA B. GREENWALD

Winner, 2025 Best Book Award, Middle East and North Africa Section, American Political Science Association

$35.00 / £30.00 paper 978-0-231-21315-8

2024 GLOBAL POLITICS

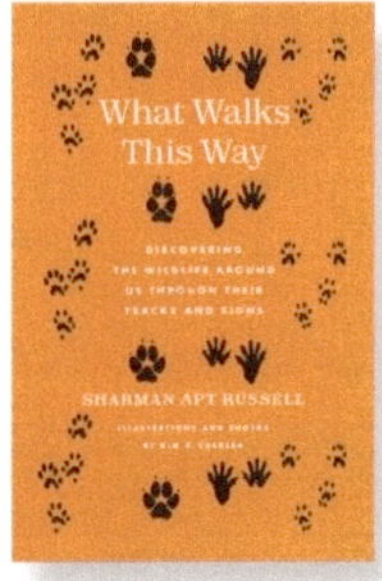

What Walks This Way

SHARMAN APT RUSSELL

Illustrations and photos by Kim A. Cabrera

Winner, 2025 New Mexico Book Awards in the category of Nature / Environment / Animals / Pets

$24.00* / £20.00 paper 978-0-231-21599-2

2024 SCIENCE

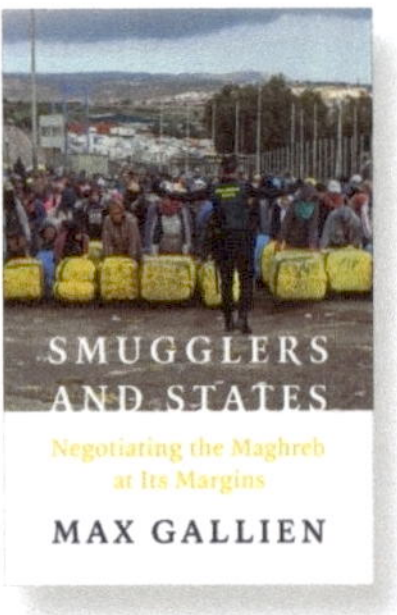

Smugglers and States

MAX GALLIEN

Winner, 2025 Theodore J. Lowi First Book Award, International Political Science Association / American Political Science Association

Winner, 2025 L. Carl Brown Book Prize, American Institute for Maghrib Studies

$35.00 / £30.00 paper 978-0-231-21289-2

2024 GLOBAL POLITICS

Writing Backwards

ALEXANDER MANSHEL

Winner, 2026 Barbara Perkins and George Perkins Prize, International Society for the Study of Narrative

Finalist, 2025 SHARP Book Prize, Society for the History of Authorship, Reading, and Publishing

$35.00 / £30.00 paper 978-0-231-21127-7

2023 LITERARY STUDIES

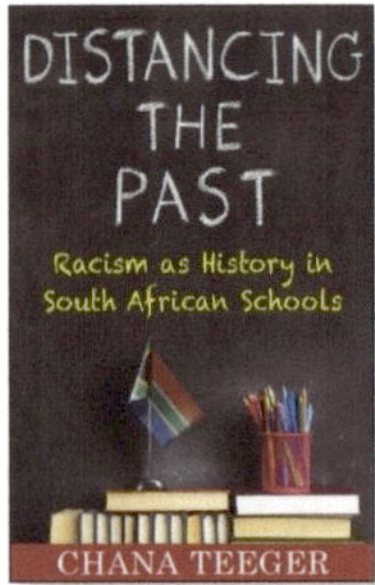

Distancing the Past

CHANA TEEGER

Winner, 2025 Gordon Hirabayashi Human Rights Book Award, Sociology of Human Rights Section, American Sociological Association

Winner, 2025 Oliver Cromwell Cox Book Award, Racial and Ethnic Minorities Section, American Sociological Association

$30.00 / £25.00 paper 978-0-231-21341-7

2024 SOCIOLOGY

Democracy and Beauty
ROBERT GOODING-WILLIAMS

$28.00* / £22.00 paper 978-0-231-22003-3
2025 PHILOSOPHY

Cooperation
BERNARD E. HARCOURT

$26.00* / £22.00 paper 978-0-231-21666-1
2023 PHILOSOPHY

The Dark Delight of Being Strange
JAMES B. HAILE III

$26.00* / £22.00 paper 978-0-231-21630-2
2024 PHILOSOPHY / LITERATURE

Shadow Work
EMILY HODGSON ANDERSON

$30.00* / £25.00 paper 978-0-231-21850-4
2025 LITERARY STUDIES

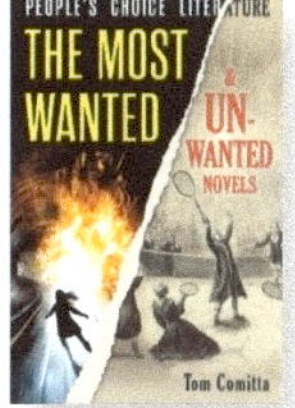

People's Choice Literature
TOM COMITTA

$25.00* / £20.00 paper 978-0-231-21928-0
2025 LITERATURE

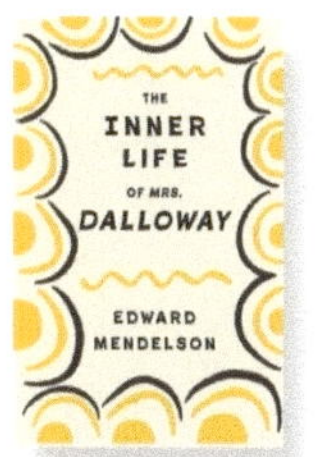

The Inner Life of *Mrs. Dalloway*
EDWARD MENDELSON

$25.00* / £20.00 paper 978-0-231-22171-9
2025 LITERARY STUDIES

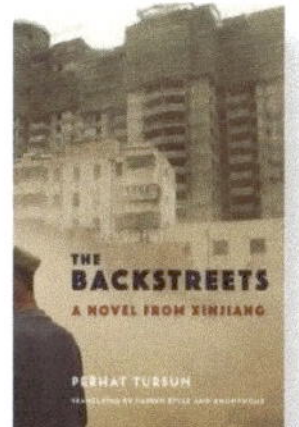

The Backstreets
PERHAT TURSUN
Translated by Darren Byler and Anonymous

$20.00* / £16.99 paper 978-0-231-20291-6
2022 FICTION IN TRANSLATION

Table for One
YUN KO-EUN
Translated by Lizzie Buehler

$20.00* / £16.99 paper 978-0-231-19203-3
2024 FICTION IN TRANSLATION

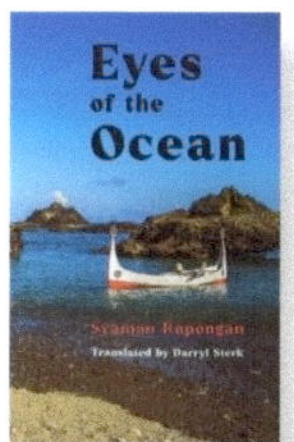

Eyes of the Ocean
SYAMAN RAPONGAN
Translated by Darryl Sterk

$28.00* / £22.00 paper 978-0-231-21979-2
2025 FICTION IN TRANSLATION

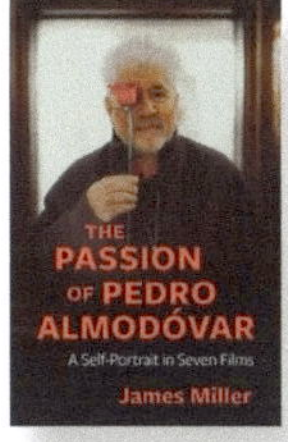

The Passion of Pedro Almodóvar
JAMES MILLER

$26.00* / £22.00 cloth 978-0-231-22004-0
2025 FILM STUDIES / PHILOSOPHY

The Sisterhood
COURTNEY THORSSON

$19.00* / £15.99 paper 978-0-231-21874-0
2023 LITERARY STUDIES

Big Fiction
DAN SINYKIN

$30.00* / £25.00 paper 978-0-231-19295-8
2023 LITERARY STUDIES

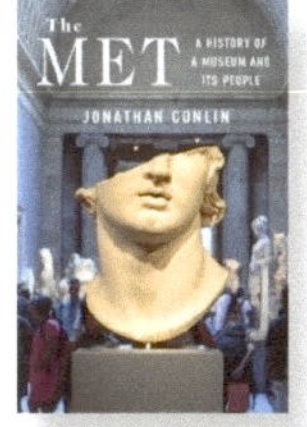

The Met
JONATHAN CONLIN

$28.00* / £22.00 paper 978-0-231-21871-9
2024 ART / NEW YORK HISTORY

Before Central Park
SARA CEDAR MILLER

$30.00* / £25.00 paper 978-0-231-18194-5
2022 NEW YORK HISTORY

Hollywood and Hitler, 1933-1939
THOMAS DOHERTY

$22.95t / £18.99 paper 978-0-231-16393-4
2013 FILM STUDIES / HISTORY

BEST OF THE BACKLIST

Vaccines and Your Family

PAUL A. OFFIT, MD, AND CHARLOTTE A. MOSER, MS

$19.95t / £16.99 paper 978-0-231-21339-4
2024 HEALTH / SCIENCE

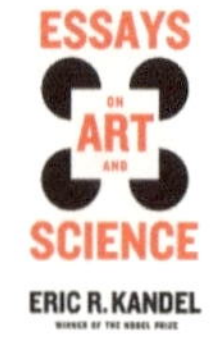

Essays on Art and Science

ERIC R. KANDEL

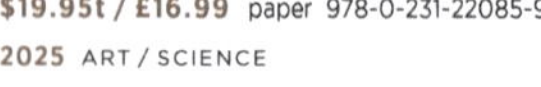
$19.95t / £16.99 paper 978-0-231-22085-9
2025 ART / SCIENCE

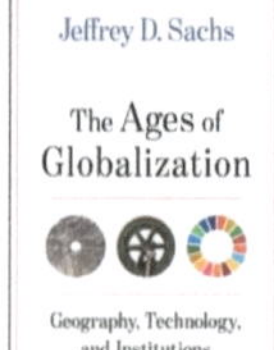

The Ages of Globalization

JEFFREY D. SACHS

$26.95t / £22.00 cloth 978-0-231-19374-0
2020 POLITICS

An Education

DIANE RAVITCH

$24.95t / £20.00 cloth 978-0-231-22029-3
2025 EDUCATION / MEMOIR

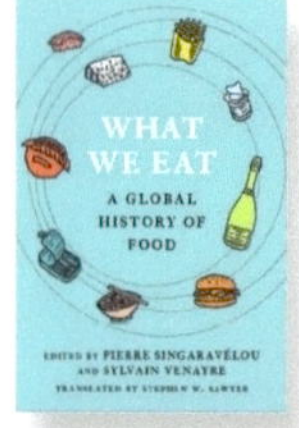

What We Eat

EDITED BY PIERRE SINGARAVÉLOU AND SYLVAIN VENAYRE

Translated by Stephen W. Sawyer

$26.00* / £22.00 paper 978-0-231-22147-4
2025 FOOD STUDIES

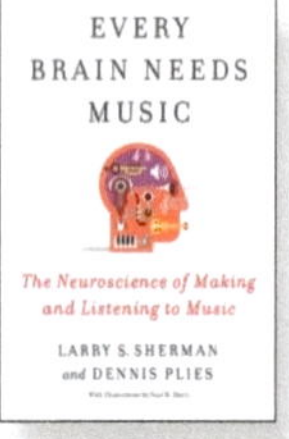

I Have No Enemies

PERRY LINK AND WU DAZHI

$28.00* / £22.00 paper 978-0-231-21676-0
2023 BIOGRAPHY

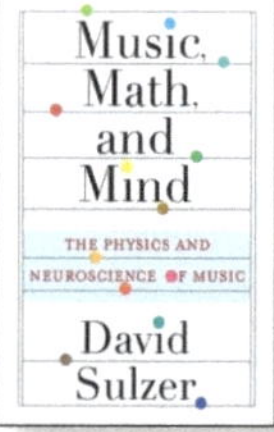

Every Brain Needs Music

LARRY S. SHERMAN AND DENNIS PLIES

$22.00* / £17.99 paper 978-0-231-21911-2
2023 SCIENCE / MUSIC

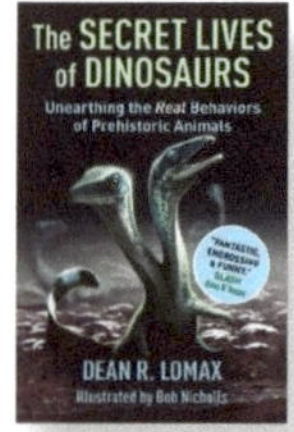

Music, Math, and Mind

DAVID SULZER

$28.00* / £22.00 paper 978-0-231-19379-5
2021 SCIENCE / MUSIC

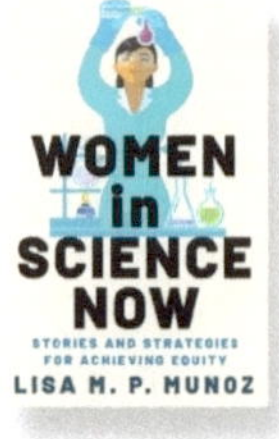

The Secret Lives of Dinosaurs

DEAN R. LOMAX

Illustrated by Bob Nicholls

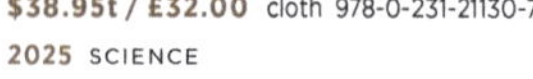
$38.95t / £32.00 cloth 978-0-231-21130-7
2025 SCIENCE

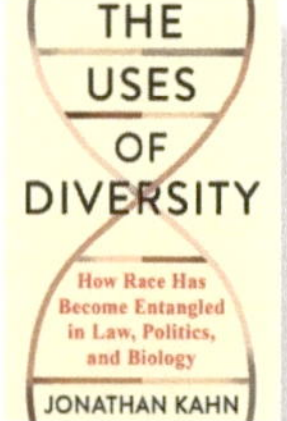

Women in Science Now

LISA M. P. MUNOZ

$19.95t / £16.99 paper 978-0-231-22084-2
2023 SCIENCE

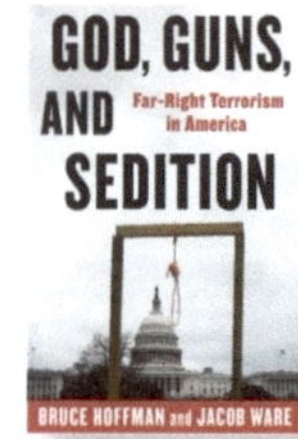

The Uses of Diversity

JONATHAN KAHN

$32.00* / £28.00 paper 978-0-231-22013-2
2025 SCIENCE

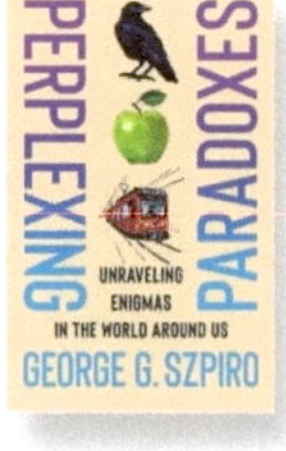

God, Guns, and Sedition

BRUCE HOFFMAN AND JACOB WARE

$22.95t / £18.99 paper 978-0-231-22069-9
2025 POLITICS

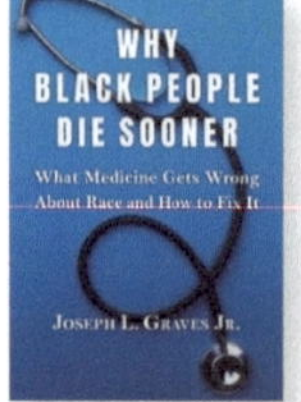

Perplexing Paradoxes

GEORGE G. SZPIRO

$35.00* / £30.00 cloth 978-0-231-21376-9
2024 SCIENCE

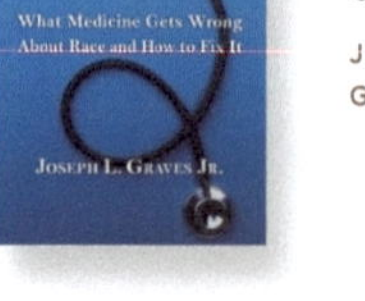

Why Black People Die Sooner

JOSEPH L. GRAVES JR.

$28.95t / £25.00 cloth 978-0-231-21796-5
2025 SCIENCE

Unreliable

CSABA SZABO

$30.00* / £25.00 paper 978-0-231-21624-1
2025 SCIENCE

AUTHOR/TITLE INDEX

CLIENT PRESSES

PLEASE CONTACT EACH PRESS DIRECTLY REGARDING EDITORIAL INQUIRIES AND RIGHTS.

AGENDA PUBLISHING LIMITED
The Core, Science Central
Beth Lane
Newcastle Upon Tyne
NE4 5TF
United Kingdom
Tel: (44) 191-495-7330
enquiries@agendapub.com
www.agendapub.com

AUSTRIAN FILM MUSEUM BOOKS
The Austrian Film Museum
Augustinerstrasse 1
A-1010 Vienna, Austria
Tel: (43) 1-533-70-54-11
www.filmmuseum.at

THE CHINESE UNIVERSITY OF HONG KONG PRESS
The Chinese University of Hong Kong
Sha Tin, New Territories, Hong Kong
Tel: (852) 3943-9800
Fax: (852) 2603-7355
cup-bus@cuhk.edu.hk
https://cup.cuhk.edu.hk/

COLUMBIA BOOKS ON ARCHITECTURE AND THE CITY
Columbia University Graduate School of Architecture, Planning, and Preservation
400 Avery Hall, 1172 Amsterdam Avenue
New York, NY 10027
Tel: (212) 851-5895
cbac@columbia.edu
www.arch.columbia.edu/books

ERIS
Lansdowne House
57 Berkeley Square
London, W1J 6ER, United Kingdom
Tel: (44) 207-870-8672
eris@eris.press
eris.press

FERNWOOD PUBLISHING
748 Broadway Ave.
Winnipeg, Manitoba, Canada
R3G 0X3

and

32 Oceanvista Lane
Black Point, Nova Scotia, Canada
B0J 1B0
(204) 474-2958
info@fernpub.ca

FLOATING OPERA PRESS
Hasenheide 9
10967 Berlin, Germany
info@floatingoperapress.com
www.floatingoperapress.com

HITCHCOCK ANNUAL
Sidney Gottlieb
Sacred Heart University
gottliebs@sacredheart.edu

IBIDEM PRESS
Melchiorstrasse 15
70439 Stuttgart, Germany
Tel: (07) 11-980-7954
Fax: (07) 11-800-1889
ibidem@ibidem-verlag.de
www.ibidemverlag.de

JAGIELLONIAN UNIVERSITY PRESS
ul. Michałowskiego 9/2
31-126 Kraków, Poland
Tel: (48) 12-663-23-80
Fax: (48) 12-663-23-83
www.wuj.pl

LINCOLN INSTITUTE OF LAND POLICY
113 Brattle Street
Cambridge, MA 02138
Tel: (617) 503-2262
publications@lincolninst.edu
www.lincolninst.edu

MARIA CURIE-SKŁODOWSKA UNIVERSITY PRESS
M. Curie-Skłodowskiej 5
30-031 Lublin, Poland
wieslaw.krajka@poczta.umcs.lublin.pl

PETERSON INSTITUTE FOR INTERNATIONAL ECONOMICS
1750 Massachusetts Ave. NW
Washington, DC 20036
Tel: (202) 328-9000
www.piie.com

ROCKBOOK
Akiko Iwamoto
aiwamoto14@rockbook.net

SOCIAL SCIENCE RESEARCH COUNCIL
One Pierrepont Plaza, 15th Floor
300 Cadman Plaza West
Brooklyn, NY 11201
Tel: (212) 377-2700
Fax: (212) 377-2727
www.ssrc.org

SUNDIAL HOUSE
Casa Hispánica
612 West 116th Street
New York, NY 10027
Tel: (212) 854-8661
SundialHouse@columbia.edu

TRANSCRIPT PUBLISHING
Hermannstrasse 26
D-33602 Bielefeld, Germany
Tel: (49) 521-39-37-9742
Fax: (49) 521-39-37-9734
order@transcript-publishing.com
www.transcript-publishing.com

TULIKA BOOKS
Indira Chandrasekhar
No. 44, first floor
Shahpur Jat, New Delhi 110 049
Tel.: (91) 11-26-49-7999, 11-26-49-1448, 11-26-49-1625
tulikadelhi@gmail.com

UNIVERSITY OF TOKYO PRESS
4-5-29 Komaba, Meguro-ku
Tokyo 153-0041, Japan
Fax: (81) 3-6407-1582
Tel: (81) 3-6407-1921
info@utp.or.jp
www.utp.or.jp

VERLAG BARBARA BUDRICH
Stauffenbergstrasse 7
D-51379 Leverkusen, Germany
Tel: (49) 021-71-34-4594
Fax: (49) 021-71-34-4693
info@budrich-academic.com

SUBAGENTS FOR COLUMBIA UNIVERSITY PRESS

ARABIC
Amélie Cherlin
Dar Cherlin
4343 Finley Ave., Apt. 3
Los Angeles, CA 90027
amelie@darcherlin.com

BRAZILIAN
Patricia Seibel
Seibel Publishing Services
Rua da Alegria, 2005, 2° E
Porto 4200-026, Portugal
patricia@patriciaseibel.com

CHINESE (SIMPLIFIED)
Ivan Zhang
Bardon-Chinese Media Agency
Room 2-702, Building 2
Rong Hua Shi Jia
No. 29, Xiao Ying Bei Lu
Chao Yang District
Beijing 100101, China
Tel: (010) 822-35383
ivan@bardonchinese.com

CHINESE (COMPLEX)
David Tsai
Bardon-Chinese Media Agency
3F, No. 150, Section 2, Roosevelt Road
Taipei, Taiwan
Tel: (886) 2-236-44995, ext. 23
david@bardonchinese.com

DUTCH AND NORDIC LANGUAGES
Paul Sebes
Sebes & Bisseling Literary Agency
Herengracht 613
1017 CE Amsterdam, Netherlands
Tel: (31) 20 616 0940
sebes@sebes.nl

FRENCH
Corinne Marotte
Marotte et Compagnie
45 rue Marx-Dormoy
F-75018 Paris, France
Tel: (33) 6-10-18-82-58
corinne@marotteetcompagnie.ag

GERMAN
Christian Dittus
Paul & Peter Fritz A.G.
Literatur Agentur
Neptunstrasse 20
8032 Zurich, Switzerland
Tel: (41) 1-388-4140
cdittus@fritzagency.com

ITALIAN
Roberto Gilodi
Reiser Literary Agency
Viale XXV Aprile 65
10133 Torino, Italy
Tel. (39) 011-5215357
roberto.gilodi@reiseragency.it

JAPANESE
Fumika Ogihara
Tuttle-Mori Agency, Inc.
Kanda Jimbocho Bldg. 4F
2-17 Kanda Jimbocho, Chiyoda-ku Tokyo
101-0051, Japan
Tel: (81) 3-3230-4083
fumika-ogihara@tuttlemori.com

Tsutomu Yawata
The English Agency (Japan) Ltd.
Sakuragi Bldg. 4F
6-7-3 Minami Aoyama, Minato-ku 107-0062 Tokyo, Japan
Tel: (81) 3-3406-5385
tsutomu_yawata@eaj.co.jp

Izumi Yoshioka
Japan UNI Agency, Inc.
1-27 Kanda Jinbo-cho, Chiyoda-ku 101-0051
Tokyo, Japan
Tel: (81) 3-3295-0301
izumi.yoshioka@japanuni.co.jp

KOREAN

Yumi Chun
Bestun Korea Agency
408 Hyoryeong-ro 53 gil 18, Seocho-gu
Seoul 06654, South Korea
Tel: (82) 2-3486-3012
bestun.ed@gmail.com

Danny Hong
Danny Hong Agency
3F, 16-12 Yanghwa-ro 12-gil, Mapo-gu
Seoul 04043, South Korea
Tel: (82) 2-6402-8890
danny@dannyhong.co.kr

Duran Kim
Duran Kim Agency
2F Taeyang Bldg.
263 Hyoryeong-r, Seocho-gu
Seoul 06653, South Korea
Tel: (82) 2-583-5724
duran@durankim.com

Joeun Lee
Korea Copyright Center Inc.
Gyonghigung Achim 3
Officetel Room 520
34, Sajik-ro 8-gil, Jongno-gu
Seoul 03174, South Korea
Tel: (82) 2-725-3350
jelee@kccseoul.com

Jackie Yang
EYA (Eric Yang Agency)
3F, e B/D, 20
Seochojungang-ro 33-gil, Seocho-gu
Seoul 06593, South Korea
Tel: (82) 2-592-3356
jackieyang@eyagency.com

POLISH
Łukasz Wróbel
GRAAL Ltd. Literary Agency
ul. Radna 12/15
00-341 Warsaw, Poland
Tel: (48) 22-828-1284
lukasz@graal.com.pl

PORTUGUESE
Gonçalo Gama Pinto
Ilídio Matos, Agência Literária Lda.
Praça Olegário Mariano, 2 - 2° Dto.
1170-278 Lisboa, Portugal
Tel: (351) 96-841-6630
goncalo.gamapinto@ilidiomatos.com

ROMANIAN AND EASTERN EUROPEAN LANGUAGES
Ioana Hodor
Livia Stoia Literary Agency
Garlei 58, Sector 1
Bucharest 013724, Romania
Tel./Fax: (40) 21 232 99 09
ioana.hodor@liviastoiaagency.ro

RUSSIAN
Alexander Korzhenevski
Igor Korzhenevski
Alexander Korzhenevski Agency
7-th Parkovaya 28-100
Moscow 105264, Russia
Tel/Fax: (7) 499-463-4412
alex.akagency@gmail.com
igor.akagency@gmail.com

SPANISH
Guillermo González
International Editors Co. (IECO)
Còrsega, 288, 1r 2a
08008 Barcelona, Spain
Tel: (34) 93-215-8812
guillermo.gonzalez@internationaleditors.com

TURKISH
Atilla Izgi Turgut
Akcali Copyright Trade
Bahariye Cad. 8/9-10
34714 Kadikoy, Istanbul, Turkey
Tel: (90) 216-338-87-71
atilla@akcalicopyright.com

GPSR Authorized Representative: Easy Access System Europe, Mustamäe tee 50, 10621 Tallinn, Estonia, gpsr.requests@easproject.com

pliance